HSK 1 Chinese Grammar

HSK 1 Chinese Grammar

A Chinese Grammar Wiki Book

Editor-in-Chief John Pasden

Foreword by Dr. David Moser

SHANGHAI

Published by AllSet Learning, Shanghai, China.

For information about educational or bulk purchases, please contact AllSet Learning at sales@allsetlearning.com.

1st print edition, 2019.

Paperback ISBN: 978-1-941875-43-8
eBook ISBN: 978-1-941875-44-5
ASID: 20190622T224718

For anyone who needs to pass the HSK
but also wants to *really learn* Chinese
and get a solid grasp of its grammar.

Table of Contents

Foreword 1

Introduction 3

HSK Levels and CEFR Levels 4

Chinese Grammar Basics for Beginners 5

HSK 1 Grammar Points: Parts of Speech

Adverbs

Expressing actions in progress with “zai” 13
(正) 在 + Verb

Negation of “you” with “mei” 15
没 + 有

Standard negation with “bu” 18
不 + Verb / Adj.

The “all” adverb “dou” 21
都 + Verb / Adj.

The “also” adverb “ye” 23
也 + Verb / Adj.

Adverbs with Adjectives

Asking about degree with “duo” 28
Subj. + 多 + Adj. ?

Expressing “not very” with “bu tai” 30
不太 + Adj.

Conjunctions

Expressing “and” with “he” 32
Noun 1 + 和 + Noun 2

Nouns

After a specific time with “yihou” 34
Time / Verb + 以后

Before a specific time with “yiqian” 36
Time / Verb + 以前

Time words and word order 38
Subj. + Time· · · · · · / Time + Subj.· · · · · ·

Numbers

Age with “sui” 40
Subj. + Number + 岁

Measure word “ge” 42
Number + 个 + Noun

Structure of dates 45
Number + 年 + Number + 月 + Number + 日

Structure of days of the week 47
星期 + Number

Structure of numbers 50
Number + Unit

Structure of times (advanced) 56
Number 1 + 点 (钟) + Number 2 + 分

Structure of times (basic) 60
Number + 点 (钟)

Particles

Expressing “not anymore” with “le” 63
不 / 没 (有) + Verb Phrase + 了

Expressing “now” with “le” 66
New Situation + 了

Expressing close possession without “de” 68
Pronoun + Noun

Expressing completion with “le” 70
Subj. + Verb + 了 + Obj.

Expressing possession with “de” 74
Noun 1 + 的 + Noun 2

Questions with “ne” 76
…… 呢 ？

Sentence-final interjection “a” 79
…… 啊

Softening speech with “ba” 82
…… 吧

Suggestions with “ba” 84
Command + 吧

Verbs

Directional verbs “lai” and “qu” 86
来 / 去 + Place

Expressing existence in a place with "zai" 88
在 + Place

Expressing existence with "you" 90
Place + 有 + Obj.

Expressing possession with "you" 92
Subj. + 有 + Obj.

Polite requests with "qing" 94
请 + Verb

Using the verb "jiao" 97
叫 + Name

Using the verb "qu" 99
去 + Place

Auxiliary verbs

Expressing "will" with "hui" 102
会 + Verb

Expressing "would like to" with "xiang" 104
想 + Verb

Expressing a learned skill with "hui" 106
会 + Verb

Expressing ability or possibility with "neng" 109
能 + Verb

Verb phrases

How to do something with "zenme" 112
怎么 + Verb ?

Indicating location with "zai" before verbs 114
Subj. + 在 + Place + Verb

Negation of past actions with "meiyou" 116
没有 + Verb

HSK 1 Grammar Points: Grammatical Structures

Basics

Basic sentence order 118
Subj. + Verb (+ Obj.)

Connecting nouns with "shi" 121
A + 是 + B

Expressing "excessively" with "tai" 124
太 + Adj. + 了

Simple “noun + adjective” sentences 126
Noun + 很 + Adj.

Noun Phrases

Expressing “some” with “yixie” 129
一些 + Noun

Numbers and Measure Words

Counting money 131
Number + 块 / 元 (+ Number + 毛 / 角) (+ 钱)

Measure words in quantity questions 134
几 + Measure Word (+ Noun) ?

Question Forms

Asking how something is with “zenmeyang” 136
…… 怎么样?

Placement of question words 138
什么 / 什么时候 / 谁 / 哪儿 / 为什么 / 怎么

Questions with “le ma” 149
Verb + 了 + 吗?

Yes-no questions with “ma” 151
…… 吗?

Sentence Patterns

The “shi… de” construction for emphasizing details 155
是…… 的

HSK 1 Grammar Points: Comparisons of Similar Grammar Points

Adverbs

Comparing “bu” and “mei” 161
不 vs 没

Keyword Index 170

Glossary 171

Acknowledgments 180

References 182

Foreword

Learning Chinese used to be a frustratingly "front-loaded" endeavor. One had to first learn pinyin, the four tones, how to write thousands of characters with the correct stroke order, how to use the 214 radicals to look up unfamiliar characters in a dictionary, and, of course, how to limn the mysterious principles of Chinese grammar. This process entailed inordinate sacrifices of eyesight, friends, and years of precious life spent "learning to learn Chinese," before the hapless student could be weaned from a diet of pre-digested pabulum and delve into the messy, glorious world of real texts.

The Chinese Grammar Wiki is on the cutting edge of a growing arsenal of digital and web resources that have made this front-loaded Sisyphean nightmare a thing of the past. This very cool tool, developed by John Pasden and the folks at AllSet Learning, is in accordance with the new "learning grammar as you go" principle of Chinese study in the digital age. Learners can now boldly embark on the ocean of Chinese very early on, with navigational tools like the Grammar Wiki to reduce the risk of getting lost at sea. For the intrepid, motivated learner, studying Chinese can now be an adventure, instead of a five-year stint in solitary confinement. And from the very outset, students can begin to move toward the goal that was formerly so elusive: the acquisition of 语感 (yǔgǎn), the "feeling for the language."

In my opinion, the Chinese Grammar Wiki has at least three very strong characteristics:

Modularity. This is a long-standing commonsense feature of website design, but it's absolutely crucial for a grammar tool like this. The Wiki has conveniently carved up Chinese grammar into useful modular chunks with the beginner in mind, so that searching for a structure or topic is intuitive, quick, and yields a clear explanation that enables the user to forge ahead, enlightened and empowered. The structure and site map is user-friendly at every level, which means that the Wiki can be easily "plugged in" to existing Chinese syllabi, or simply employed by the student independently to explore texts and materials outside of class.

Interlinking. The Wiki is structured so that alongside the grammar points on most pages there are helpful links to related or similar grammar points within the Wiki. For example, in exploring the grammatical points for 比 (bǐ) involving comparison, you will find explanations of the basic 比 (bǐ) structure, examples, and common errors, but in addition you will also see links to other "comparison" structures using 没有 (méiyǒu). This interlinking feature gives the user a fuller picture of various grammatical structures that serve similar functions in the language.

Universality. One of the strongest points of the Chinese Grammar Wiki is that the grammatical explanations have been tailored so as to contain the right amount of information, at the right level of specificity and complexity for the majority of learners. Designing a grammar resource with such wide applicability is not an easy task, requiring not only technical know-how and careful thinking, but also a strong intuitive sense of what the average student needs to know. Linguist Edward Sapir said "all grammars leak," and this mutable, watery quality of language means that no grammatical framework is going to contain only tidy, airtight rules that cover every situation. In explanations, there is always a tradeoff between succinct simplicity and the real-life complexity, and the Wiki does an admirable job of striking a satisfying balance between these two yin-yang poles.

Being digital in nature, the Chinese Grammar Wiki is very much a work in progress, and the designers always welcome input and suggestions. Product development is always an interactive process, and the more people use the resource, the more useful it will become. I encourage Chinese students at all levels – and even Chinese teachers – to check it out and discover what the reference tools of the 21st century will look like.

No matter what well-meaning pedagogical Pollyannas might tell you, Chinese is still "damn hard." Thankfully, there now are digital resources like the Chinese Grammar Wiki, which goes a long way to making the struggle easier.

David Moser
Academic Director, CET Beijing Chinese Studies
Beijing Capital Normal University

Introduction

The **Chinese Grammar Wiki** began life as an Excel spreadsheet full of grammar points organized by difficulty level. This list was needed to track the progress of AllSet Learning's clients and to design personalized grammar practice where it was most needed. But as the lists continued to grow and evolve, it quickly became apparent that it made sense to put the grammar points online, so that the newest version would always be front and center. For ease of editing, what could be better than a wiki? And if AllSet Learning teachers were to have access, why not open up access to *all learners*? The Chinese Grammar Wiki was developed internally for about a year before becoming public in January of 2012. Since then, it has grown tremendously, both in content and in traffic.

Probably the most important feature of the Chinese Grammar Wiki, which has always been kept at the forefront of its development, is its focus on learner level. An absolute beginner can't absorb a multitude of uses for every grammar point she encounters, and she shouldn't be expected to. And she certainly shouldn't be given frustratingly difficult example sentences when trying to grasp the most basic grammar concepts. That's why example sentences on the Chinese Grammar Wiki are plentiful, but relentlessly edited to be level-appropriate. And for the learners that can't get enough, relevant articles of all levels are always just a link away. Although the wiki aims to be 100% comprehensive, it's no coincidence that there are fewer A1 grammar points than A2 grammar points, and fewer A2 grammar points than B1 grammar points. Considerable thought and care has gone into curating and pruning the lists of grammar points.

The Chinese Grammar Wiki is not a Chinese course. Rather, it is a companion resource that can complement any Chinese class. Don't expect to read it from start to finish, or to go through the grammar point lists from top to bottom. But do expect to come back often. And expect to get sucked into the curiously logical world of Chinese grammar.

John Pasden
Editor-in-Chief and CEO
AllSet Learning, Shanghai, China

HSK Levels and CEFR Levels

Since the company's inception in 2010, AllSet Learning has used the Common European Framework of Reference (CEFR) levels for its clients and study materials. CEFR has a great reputation for being practical and descriptive of communicative proficiency (we especially like the "Can Do" statements) while mercifully keeping the leveling and sub-leveling to a minimum. The A1-A2, B1-B2, C1-C2 progression is intuitive and helpful for both learners and educators, and can also be fairly easily converted to the American ACTFL level system.

The current version of the HSK (*Hanyu Shuiping Kaoshi*) dates back to 2010, and was last revised in 2012. It consists of six levels (1-6), and was designed, in part, to correspond to the six CEFR levels. European Chinese language teachers have reported that the correspondence, in practice, is somewhat different, with HSK 6 actually matching no higher than the CEFR B2-C1 level range. Furthermore, the HSK levels are used more as a standard for academic requirements (e.g. being admitted to an undergraduate or graduate program in China) rather than real-life application (the above-mentioned "communicative proficiency").

Our conclusion is that while both leveling systems clearly have their uses, it is not possible to equally accommodate both systems in one list of grammar points. That is why the Chinese Grammar Wiki has created separate listings for CEFR levels and HSK levels. We encourage test-takers of the HSK to refer to the HSK level lists, while learners focused more on real-life communication can benefit more from the CEFR levels. This book focuses on the HSK levels.

Chinese Grammar Basics for Beginners

As a beginner, Chinese grammar can be challenging to understand. In this quick overview, we will provide you with some basic information on Chinese grammar as well as some good starting points.

Background

English is classified as an Indo-European language. This language family includes a lot of languages spoken in the western world, including the romance languages (such as Spanish, French, and Portuguese) as well as the Slavic languages (such as Russian, Czech, and Polish), and many others. All of these languages have common grammatical features which include conjugating verbs for different tenses, following specific rules about subject-verb agreement, and adding endings to words to make them plural.

Chinese is not part of the Indo-European family at all. Instead, it is classified as a Sino-Tibetan language, and, unsurprisingly, its grammar is quite different from the grammar of those European languages you may have encountered before. Still, Chinese grammar may surprise you with its pleasing simplicity and consistent logical structure.

As a language, Chinese (quote famously) does not have an alphabet. Instead, characters known as "*hanzi*" (汉字) are used to express the different sounds of the language. These characters can also be written using the roman letters in a system called "pinyin." All beginners should learn pinyin first. Pinyin is provided for all Chinese characters that appear in A1 and A2 grammar points.

The Basics

There are a number of misconceptions about Chinese grammar, the most egregious being that "Chinese has no grammar." If Mandarin Chinese truly had *no grammar*, you could make no grammar mistakes, and no learners would ever struggle with it. We will start this overview by looking at some specific areas of Chinese grammar that can sometimes trip up beginners.

Word Order

For many simple cases, the basic sentence structure[1] of Chinese is the same in Chinese as it is in English. Both languages use a subject-verb or subject-verb-object (SVO) formula for making simple sentences. This familiar pattern means that you shouldn't have much trouble with word order at first.

1. Basic sentence order (Grammar), page 118

Subject-Verb Examples:

Subject	Verb	Translation
你 Nǐ	吃。 chī.	You eat.
他 Tā	笑。 xiào.	He laughs.
我 Wǒ	去。 qù.	I go.

Subject-Verb-Object Examples:

Subject	Verb	Object	Translation
我 Wǒ	吃 chī.	肉。 ròu.	I eat meat.
你 Nǐ	喝 hē	水。 shuǐ.	You drink water.
他 Tā	说 shuō	中文。 Zhōngwén.	He speaks Chinese.

More examples can be found on our basic word order[1] page.

As sentences get more complex, you'll note that Chinese word order does, in fact, diverge significantly from English word order, even for some relatively simple sentences. For help with those, check out our articles on time words[2], locations of actions[3], using simple adverbs correctly[4], and making simple noun-adjective sentences[5].

Questions

Simple sentences can be turned into yes/no questions by adding 吗 (ma) to the end of simple statements. For each of the following, you could make a simple statement by dropping 吗 (ma).

---

1. Basic sentence order (Grammar), page 118
2. Time words and word order (Grammar), page 38
3. Indicating location with "zai" before verbs (Grammar), page 114
4. The "also" adverb "ye" (Grammar), page 23
5. Simple "noun + adjective" sentences (Grammar), page 126

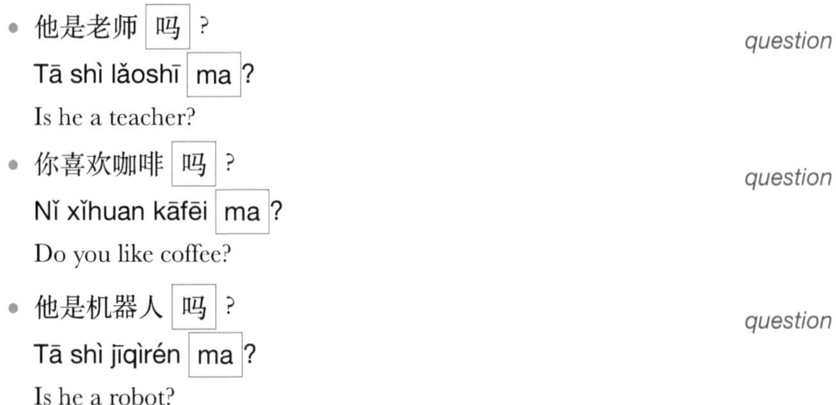

- 他是老师 吗 ?
  Tā shì lǎoshī ma ?
  Is he a teacher? *question*
- 你喜欢咖啡 吗 ?
  Nǐ xǐhuan kāfēi ma ?
  Do you like coffee? *question*
- 他是机器人 吗 ?
  Tā shì jīqìrén ma ?
  Is he a robot? *question*

Another important question particle for beginners to understand is 呢 (ne)[1]. 呢 (ne) is simply added after a topic to turn it into a "what about...?" question. This is useful in conversations to say things like "what about you?" or "what about my money?" This particle is simply tagged onto a subject to form the question.

- 我吃饭了。你 呢 ?
  Wǒ chīfàn le. Nǐ ne ?
  I've eaten. What about you?
- 北京下雨了。上海 呢 ?
  Běijīng xià yǔ le. Shànghǎi ne ?
  It's raining in Beijing. How about Shanghai?
- 你说他们可以去。我们 呢 ?
  Nǐ shuō tāmen kěyǐ qù. Wǒmen ne ?
  You said they can go. What about us?

There are of course other ways to form questions[2]. In English, we use question words, commonly referred to as the "5 W's and 1 H" (what, where, who, when, why, how), to make questions. These question words also exist in Chinese, but their placement within a sentence in Chinese is different from English. The structure of a question in Chinese follows the same structure as a normal statement.

For example, in English the structure of the question "Who are you?" puts the question word "who" at the beginning of the sentence. If the person answering this question says, "I am Li Li" we can see that the answer to the question comes at the end of the sentence. In Chinese, the structure of the question to learn someone's name is "You are who?" So the question follows the same structure as the answer (subject-verb-object). This works for all kinds of other

---

1. Questions with "ne" (Grammar), page 76
2. Placement of question words (Grammar), page 138

questions too. For example, in Chinese, to ask "What is it?" you literally say, "It is what?"

- 什么
  shénme
  what
- 哪里 / 哪儿
  nǎlǐ / nǎr
  where
- 谁
  shéi
  who
- 什么时候
  shénme shíhou
  when
- 为什么
  wèishénme
  why
- 怎么
  zěnme
  how

Possession

Possession can be shown using the particle 的 (de)[1]. This character functions the same way as an apostrophe-"s" does in English and is added after the "owner," before the "thing owned." One interesting result of this extremely versatile system is that you don't need separate words for "my" or "your" or "his"; you just follow the words for "I" or "you" or "he" with a 的 (de).

- 小李 的 手机
  Xiǎo Lǐ de shǒujī
  Xiao Li's cell phone
- 我 的 手机
  Wǒ de shǒujī
  My cell phone

1. Expressing possession with "de" (Grammar), page 74

- 公司 的 老板

  gōngsī de lǎobǎn

  the company's boss

- 他 的 小狗

  Tā de xiǎogǒu

  His puppy

Possession can also be expressed with 有 (yǒu)[1], the Chinese verb meaning "to have." Just like we can say in English "I have the tickets" or "she has the camera," 有 (yǒu) can indicate this type of possession.

- 我 有 钱。

  Wǒ yǒu qián.

  I have money.

- 他 有 两个女儿。

  Tā yǒu liǎng gè nǚér.

  He has two daughters.

- 你 有 工作吗?

  Nǐ yǒu gōngzuò ma?

  Do you have a job?

Negation

The same basic word order holds true when using the negative. Simply put the word 不 (bù)[2] before verbs[2] and adjectives[2]. This functions much like the word "not" in English.

- 我 不 喝酒 。

  bù hējiǔ.

  She doesn't drink alcohol.

- 他们 不 想工作 。

  Tāmen bù xiǎng gōngzuò .

  They don't want to work.

- 她 不 漂亮 。

  Tā bù piàoliang .

  She is not pretty.

---

1. Expressing possession with "you" (Grammar), page 92
2. Standard negation with "bu" (Grammar), page 18

When talking about what you do not "have," you use the word 没 (méi)[1] instead of 不 (bu). It is placed right before the verb 有 (yǒu)[2] to form the "do not have" phrase 没有 (méiyǒu)[1]. This allows you to say sentences like "Walter doesn't have a car" or "Voltron doesn't have the books."

- 我 没 有 手机。

  Wǒ méi yǒu shǒujī.

  I don't have a cell phone.

- 我们 没 有 房子。

  Wǒmen méi yǒu fángzi.

  We don't have a house.

- 他们公司 没 有 电脑。

  Tāmen gōngsī méi yǒu diànnǎo.

  Their company doesn't have computers.

Aspect

As we mentioned already, there is a silly notion floating around that Chinese has no grammar. While this belief is false, it probably stems from the fact Chinese has no formal tenses to express events that took place in either the past or the future. Instead of tense, the language makes use of time words[3] and puts more emphasis on aspect. You don't need to worry about this in the beginning; just remember to use time words to make clear when something happened, and the aspect thing will come with time. (Hint: aspect involves the particle 了 (le), which you'll be spending more time with later.)

Parts of Speech

All words can be classified into parts of speech to define what roles the words play in sentences. Here, we will briefly recap how these different parts of speech work in English, and explain how the same rules apply to Chinese grammar.

Nouns are commonly referred to as "person, place, or thing" words. As you start learning more Chinese vocabulary, many of the words you will learn will be nouns. These will make up the subjects and the objects of the sentences you study.

Verbs are words that describe actions (sometimes mental or abstract rather than physical). Chinese does not conjugate verbs. Chinese verbs stay the same, regardless of when the action takes place or who performs it.

---

1. Negation of "you" with "mei" (Grammar), page 15
2. Expressing possession with "you" (Grammar), page 92
3. Time words and word order (Grammar), page 38

Here are some good verbs for beginners to start learning:

- 是 (shì) - verb for "to be"[1]
- 在 (zài) - verb for "to be located"[2]
- 有 (yǒu) - verb for "there is / there are"[3]
- 叫 (jiào) - verb for "to be called"[4]
- 去 (qù) - verb for "to go"[5]

Adverbs are words that modify verbs and adjectives. In Chinese, the adverb *always* goes *before* the verb or adjective. Instead of saying "I run also," proper grammar in Chinese would be "I also run." It's very consistent in Chinese.

Here are some good adverbs for beginners to start learning:

- 都 (dōu) - adverb for "all"[6]
- 也 (yě) - adverb for "also"[7]
- 太 (tài) - adverb for "too," as in "excessively"[8]

Adjectives are words that describe nouns. Chinese has some unique rules about how adjectives interact with different nouns and verbs.

Here are some good adjective rules for beginners to start learning:

- Simple sentences with adjectives[9]
- 是 (shì) - the verb for "to be"[1]

Conjunctions are words that join two thoughts together in a sentence. The three most common ones in English are "and," "but," and "or." As you learn more about these conjunctions in Chinese, you will discover that they're each a little different from their English equivalents.

Here are some good conjunctions for beginners to start learning:

- 和 (hé) - conjunction for "and"[10]
- 还是 (háishì) - conjunction for "or"

---

1. Connecting nouns with "shi" (Grammar), page 121
2. Expressing existence in a place with "zai" (Grammar), page 88
3. Expressing existence with "you" (Grammar), page 90
4. Using the verb "jiao" (Grammar), page 97
5. Using the verb "qu" (Grammar), page 99
6. The "all" adverb "dou" (Grammar), page 21
7. The "also" adverb "ye" (Grammar), page 23
8. Expressing "excessively" with "tai" (Grammar), page 124
9. Simple "noun + adjective" sentences (Grammar), page 126
10. Expressing "and" with "he" (Grammar), page 32

Articles are kind of a confusing concept in English, but the main English articles are "a," "an," and "the." We use them when saying things like "I have a laptop" or "open the door." In Chinese, articles *don't exist*. There is no word for "a" or "the" in Chinese.

Numbers are the words we use to express specific quantities. We use numbers to express value, time, and other important functions in our lives. They can be used for all of these same functions in Chinese.

Here are some good number structures for beginners to start learning.

- Structure of numbers[1]
- Structure of times[2]
- Structure of days of the week[3]
- Structure of dates[4]

Measure words are words that pair up with numbers and help describe the nouns that are being counted (or "measured"). We don't have such a pervasive, complete system for this in English, but we do something similar when we say, "5 pieces of pizza" or "3 sheets of paper."

Here is the only measure word beginners need to start learning the concept:

- Measure word 个 (gè)[5]

Ready for more?

Of course all of this is just the beginning. There are many more interesting grammar patterns that can help you correctly express lots of different things in Chinese. Take a look at the A1 grammar points for more beginner-friendly grammar help. Just keep in mind that these grammar points are not sequential. Start with what you need help with most, and branch out from there.

---

1. Structure of numbers (Grammar), page 50
2. Structure of times (basic) (Grammar), page 60
3. Structure of days of the week (Grammar), page 47
4. Structure of dates (Grammar), page 45
5. Measure word "ge" (Grammar), page 42

Expressing actions in progress with "zai"

在 (zài) and 正在 (zhèngzài) can be used as auxiliary verbs to express that an action is *ongoing* or *in progress*. This is often the equivalent of *present continuous* in English, which is how we express that an activity is happening *now*.

You can use 正在 (zhèngzài) instead of just 在 (zài) to put a little more emphasis on an action that is *in progress* ***right now***.

Structure

 Subj. + 在 + Verb + Obj.

or

 Subj. + 正在 + Verb + Obj.

Examples

- 她 在 看书。
  Tā zài kànshū.
  She is reading.
- 妈妈 在 打电话。
  Māma zài dǎ diànhuà.
  Mom is making a phone call.
- 谁 在 里面洗澡?
  Shéi zài lǐmiàn xǐzǎo?
  Who is taking a shower in there?
- 阿姨 正在 打扫我们的房间。
  Āyí zhèngzài dǎsǎo wǒmen de fángjiān.
  The cleaning lady is cleaning our room right now.

- 昨天晚上七点，我们 在 吃饭。
  Zuótiān wǎnshang qīdiǎn, wǒmen zài chīfàn.
  Yesterday at 7pm, we were eating dinner.
- 老板 在 开会，没有时间见你。
  Lǎobǎn zài kāihuì, méiyǒu shíjiān jiàn nǐ.
  The boss is currently in a meeting. He doesn't have time to see you.
- 我现在 在 上班，不方便离开。
  Wǒ xiànzài zài shàngbān, bù fāngbiàn líkāi.
  I am working now. It's not convenient for me to leave.
- 我们 正在 上课，请你等一会儿。
  Wǒmen zhèngzài shàngkè, qǐng nǐ děng yīhuìr.
  We are in class right now; please wait a moment.
- 你 正在 开车，不可以玩手机。
  Nǐ zhèngzài kāichē, bù kěyǐ wán shǒujī.
  You're driving right now; you can't play with your cell phone.
- 你给我打电话的时候，我 正在 跟朋友打游戏。
  Nǐ gěi wǒ dǎ diànhuà de shíhou, wǒ zhèngzài gēn péngyou dǎ yóuxì.
  When you called me, I was playing video games with friends.

There is no need to worry too much about when to use 在 (zài) or 正在 (zhèngzài), since they basically mean the same thing. 正在 (zhèngzài) usually shows that the action is in progress (*right now*). "在 (zài) + Verb" is more commonly used than "正在 (zhèngzài) + Verb," but both are fine to use.

Similar to

- Aspect particle "zhe" (HSK2, HSK3)

Negation of "you" with "mei"

The verb 有 (yǒu) is negated differently from ordinary verbs. Rather than placing 不 (bù) before it as with other verbs, you must use 没 (méi) to negate the verb 有 (yǒu).

Structure

Nearly all verbs can be negated with 不 (bù)[1]. The verb 有 (yǒu) is an important exception to this rule, and must be negated with 没 (méi).

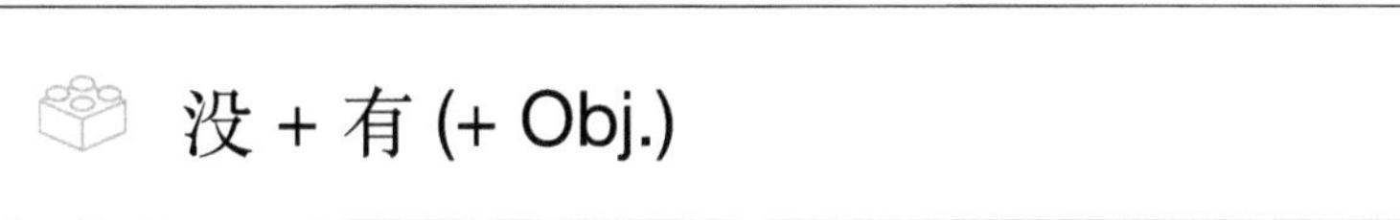

Note: because of the special relationship between 没 (méi) and 有 (yǒu), the pinyin for 没有 is normally written without a space: "méiyǒu."

Examples

- 我 没有 问题。
  Wǒ méiyǒu wèntí.
  I don't have any questions.
- 我们现在 没有 钱。
  Wǒmen xiànzài méiyǒu qián.
  We don't have money now.
- 他 没有 工作吗?
  Tā méiyǒu gōngzuò ma?
  Does he not have a job?
- 他们 没有 爸爸妈妈。
  Tāmen méiyǒu bàba māma.
  They don't have parents.
- 我们在北京 没有 房子。
  Wǒmen zài Běijīng méiyǒu fángzi.
  We don't have a house in Beijing.

---

1. Standard negation with "bu" (Grammar), page 18

- 你爸爸 没有 手机吗?
  Nǐ bàba méiyǒu shǒujī ma?
  Does your dad not have a cell phone?
- 你们在上海 没有 朋友吗?
  Nǐmen zài Shànghǎi méiyǒu péngyou ma?
  Do you not have friends in Shanghai?
- 我的老师现在 没有 男朋友。
  Wǒ de lǎoshī xiànzài méiyǒu nánpéngyou.
  My teacher doesn't have a boyfriend now.
- 他们都 没有 电脑吗?
  Tāmen dōu méiyǒu diànnǎo ma?
  Do they all not have computers?
- 这个周末你们都 没有 时间吗?
  Zhège zhōumò nǐmen dōu méiyǒu shíjiān ma?
  Do you all not have time this weekend?

Remember that trying to negate 有 (yǒu) with 不 (bù) is a classic mistake that many people make in the early stages of studying Chinese:

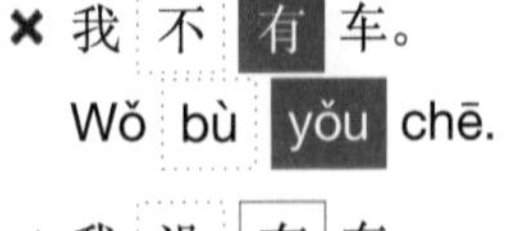

✗ 我 不 有 车。
Wǒ bù yǒu chē.

Never use 不 with 有!

✓ 我 没 有 车。
Wǒ méi yǒu chē.
I don't have a car.

Always use 没 with 有.

Never use 不 (bù) with 有 (yǒu).

The Short Form of 没有 (méiyǒu) is 没 (méi)

没有 (méiyǒu) can be shortened to 没 (méi) without altering its meaning.

- 我 没 钱。
  Wǒ méi qián.
  I don't have money.
- 你 没 男朋友吗?
  Nǐ méi nánpéngyou ma?
  Do you not have a boyfriend?

- 你们 没 车吗?
  Nǐmen méi chē ma?
  You don't have a car?
- 老板现在 没 时间。
  Lǎobǎn xiànzài méi shíjiān.
  The boss doesn't have time right now.
- 我 没 工作，我老公也 没 工作。
  Wǒ méi gōngzuò, wǒ lǎogōng yě méi gōngzuò.
  I don't have a job. My husband doesn't have a job either.

Similar to

- Comparing "bu" and "mei" (HSK1), page 161
- Expressing existence with "you" (HSK1), page 90
- Expressing possession with "you" (HSK1), page 92
- Negation of past actions with "meiyou" (HSK1), page 116
- Standard negation with "bu" (HSK1), page 18
- Basic comparisons with "meiyou" (HSK3)
- Expressing "no" (noun) "to" (verb) with "wu… ke…" (HSK5)

Standard negation with “bu”

不 (bù) is generally used to negate a verb in the present or future, or to talk about what you do not do, as a habit. So expressing things like “I don’t want to go” or “I’m not going” or “I don’t eat meat” would be typical uses of 不 (bù).

Negating Verbs

Structure

The standard way to negate verbs in Chinese is with 不 (bù). To negate a verb, simply place 不 (bù) before it:

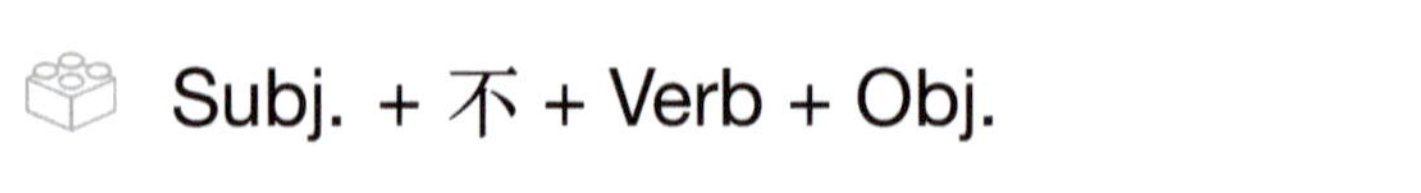

Examples

- 他们 不 是 坏孩子。
  Tāmen bù shì huài háizi.
  They are not bad kids.
- 我们 不 喝 酒。
  Wǒmen bù hē jiǔ.
  We don't drink alcohol.
- 我今天 不 想工作 。
  Wǒ jīntiān bù xiǎng gōngzuò .
  I don't want to work today.
- 你 不 喜欢 我吗?
  Nǐ bù xǐhuan wǒ ma?
  Do you not like me?
- 为什么你 不 喜欢喝 咖啡?
  Wèishénme nǐ bù xǐhuan hē kāfēi?
  Why don't you like to drink coffee?

Almost all verbs can be negated with 不 (bù) (unless you’re talking about the past[1]). The only verb that can never be negated with 不 (bù) is 有 (yǒu)[2].

- ✘ 我 不 有 时间。
  Wǒ bù yǒu shíjiān.
- ✔ 我 没 有 时间。
  Wǒ méi yǒu shíjiān.
  I don't have time.

Negating Adjectives

As it turns out, the structure with an adjective is basically the same as the one with a verb.

Structure

Subj. + 不 + Adj.

Examples

- 我 不 饿 。
  Wǒ bù è .
  I'm not hungry.
- 这个 不 贵 。
  Zhège bù guì .
  This is not expensive.
- 公司 不 大 。
  Gōngsī bù dà .
  The company is not big.
- 老板今天很 不 高兴 。
  Lǎobǎn jīntiān hěn bù gāoxìng .
  The boss is very unhappy today.

---

1. Negation of past actions with "meiyou" (Grammar), page 116
2. Negation of "you" with "mei" (Grammar), page 15

- 我哥哥 不 高 ，但是很帅。
  Wǒ gēge bù gāo , dànshì hěn shuài.
  My older brother is not tall, but he is very handsome.

Similar to

- Comparing “bu” and “mei” (HSK1), page 161
- Connecting nouns with “shi” (HSK1), page 121
- Negation of “you” with “mei” (HSK1), page 15
- Negation of past actions with “meiyou” (HSK1), page 116

The “all” adverb “dou”

The adverb 都 (dōu) is used to express “all” in Chinese. It’s common to use 都 (dōu) in a variety of sentences where it would seem unnecessary in English.

都 (dōu) for “All”

Structure

 Subj. + 都 + [Verb Phrase]

Remember that 都 (dōu) appears *after* the subject. A common mistake learners make is to put 都 (dōu) at the beginning of the sentence (as “all” often appears there in English). This isn’t good Chinese - make sure you put 都 (dōu) after the subject and before the verb.

Examples

- 你们 都 认识 John 吗?
  Nǐmen dōu rènshi John ma?
  Do you all know John?
- 他们 都 在上海。
  Tāmen dōu zài Shànghǎi.
  They are all in Shanghai.
- 明天我们 都 可以去。
  Míngtiān wǒmen dōu kěyǐ qù.
  Tomorrow we all can go.
- 你们 都 用 wiki 吗?
  Nǐmen dōu yòng wiki ma?
  Do you all use the wiki?
- 我们 都 要冰水。
  Wǒmen dōu yào bīngshuǐ .
  We all want ice water.

都 (dōu) for "Both"

Chinese doesn't normally use a special word for "both" like English does. It just uses 都 (dōu) as if it were any other number greater than one. Chinese also doesn't have a special pattern like "neither / nor" for the negative case. Just use 都 (dōu) and make the sentence negative.

Structure

This pattern should look familiar.

Examples

These examples follow exactly the same form in Chinese as the ones above. The only difference is that here we don't translate 都 (dōu) as "all" in English; we translate it as "both," and for negative cases, we translate it as "neither."

- 我们两个 都 爱你。
  Wǒmen liǎng gè dōu ài nǐ.
  The two of us both love you.
- 你爸爸和你妈妈 都 是美国人吗?
  Nǐ bàba hé nǐ māma dōu shì Měiguó rén ma?
  Are your father and your mother both Americans?
- 我和我太太 都 不吃肉。
  Wǒ hé wǒ tàitai dōu bù chī ròu.
  Neither my wife nor I eat meat.
- 你们两个 都 喜欢中国菜吗?
  Nǐmen liǎng gè dōu xǐhuan Zhōngguó cài ma?
  Do you both like Chinese food?
- 她和她老公 都 没有工作。
  Tā hé tā lǎogōng dōu méiyǒu gōngzuò.
  Neither she nor her husband has a job.

Similar to

- Emphasizing quantity with "dou" (HSK2)

The "also" adverb "ye"

The English adverb "too" or "also" is expressed in Chinese as 也 (yě). In Chinese, it *always* needs to come before the verb (or adjective).

也 (yě) with Verb Phrases

Structure

Since it is an adverb, 也 (yě) is inserted after the subject, before the verb or verb phrase.

 Subj. + 也 + Verb / [Verb Phrase]

Examples

- 我 也 喜欢。
  Wǒ yě xǐhuan.
  I also like it.
- 我 也 是学生。
  Wǒ yě shì xuésheng.
  I am a student too.
- 她 也 有一个儿子。
  Tā yě yǒu yī gè érzi.
  She also has a son.
- 他们 也 是法国人吗?
  Tāmen yě shì Fǎguó rén ma?
  Are they also French?
- 我 也 想学中文。
  Wǒ yě xiǎng xué Zhōngwén.
  I also want to study Chinese.
- 他们 也 会去吗?
  Tāmen yě huì qù ma?
  Are they also going?

- 我妈妈 也 喜欢吃饺子。
  Wǒ māma yě xǐhuan chī jiǎozi.
  My mother likes to eat boiled dumplings too.
- 孩子 也 可以喝酒吗?
  Háizi yě kěyǐ hējiǔ ma?
  Can kids drink alcohol too?
- 你 也 想来我家吗?
  Nǐ yě xiǎng lái wǒ jiā ma?
  Do you want to come to my house too?
- 她 也 觉得这个老师不好。
  Tā yě juéde zhège lǎoshī bù hǎo.
  She also thinks this teacher isn't good.

Let's take one more look at two different English sentences which mean the same thing, but can result in bad Chinese if you translate word-for-word.

✔ 我 也 喜欢 。
Wǒ yě xǐhuan .
I also like it.

✖ 我 喜欢 也 。
Wǒ xǐhuan yě.
I like it too.

Note that the translation for the first sentence is "I also like it." The translation of the second sentence is "I like it too," which is equally correct in English, but translated word-for-word into Chinese, the 也 (yě) comes at the end of the sentence, which is *100% wrong* in Chinese.

A Note on the Negative Form

Please note that in English, we replace the word "too" with "either" in negative sentences. For example:

A: I like cats.

B: I like cats *too*.

A: I *don't* like cats.

B: I don't like cats *either*.

In Chinese, regardless of whether the sentence is positive ("I like them **too**") or negative ("I **don't** like them **either**"), 也 (yě) is used the same way. Just make sure you put the 也 (yě) *before* the 不 (bù) or other negative part that comes before the verb.

- 我 也 不 喜欢。
  Wǒ yě bù xǐhuan.
  I don't like it either.
- 我 也 不 知道。
  Wǒ yě bù zhīdào.
  I don't know either.
- 他 也 没 有。
  Tā yě méiyǒu.
  He doesn't have it either.
- 你 也 不 想来我家吗?
  Nǐ yě bù xiǎng lái wǒ jiā ma?
  You don't want to come to my house either?

也 (yě) with Adjectives

Structure

也 (yě) can also be used with adjectives. Remember that for simple "noun + adjective" sentences[1] you normally need to include an adverb like 很 (hěn) before the adjective. In that case, just put the 也 (yě) before the adverb.

 Subj. + 也 (+ Adv.) + Adj.

Examples

- 你 也 很 高。
  Nǐ yě hěn gāo.
  You are also tall.
- 他 也 很 胖。
  Tā yě hěn pàng.
  He is also fat.

1. Simple "noun + adjective" sentences (Grammar), page 126

- 我爸爸 也 很 帅。
  Wǒ bàba yě hěn shuài.
  My dad is also handsome.
- 湖南菜 也 很 辣。
  Húnán cài yě hěn là.
  Hunan food is very spicy too.
- 这种酒 也 很 好喝。
  Zhè zhǒng jiǔ yě hěn hǎohē.
  This kind of alcohol is also good.
- 这个地方 也 很 漂亮。
  Zhège dìfang yě hěn piàoliang.
  This place is also pretty.
- 昨天很冷，今天 也 很 冷。
  Zuótiān hěn lěng, jīntiān yě hěn lěng.
  Yesterday was cold, and today is also cold.
- 他生气了？我 也 很 生气！
  Tā shēngqì le? Wǒ yě hěn shēngqì!
  He got angry? I'm also angry!
- 这个问题 也 很 麻烦。
  Zhège wèntí yě hěn máfan.
  This problem is also very troublesome.
- 我觉得这个餐厅 也 很 好。
  Wǒ juéde zhège cāntīng yě hěn hǎo.
  I think that this restaurant is also good.

Expressing "Me Too" with 也 (yě)

It can be tricky to know how to say "me too" when you first study 也 (yě), as you can't say "wǒ yě" all by itself. That's not a complete sentence; you can't just leave 也 (yě) hanging there with nothing after it.

The all-purpose correct sentence is "wǒ yě shì," which literally means, "I am too," but can also stand in for "me too."

Structure

The correct structure uses the verb 是 (shì):

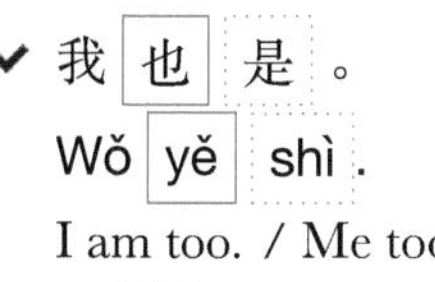

✔ 我 也 是 。

Wǒ yě shì .

I am too. / Me too.

The 是 fills in for whatever was just said.

✘ 我 也 。

Wǒ yě.

Always put something after 也! It never ends a sentence.

Examples

The "me too" structure works with other subjects, as well. But for these simple examples, we'll stick to the classic 我 (wǒ) subject.

A: 我是美国人。

Wǒ shì Měiguó rén.

I am an American.

B: 我 也 是 。

Wǒ yě shì .

Me too. / I am too.

For this next one, you'll notice that the "me too" reply repeats the original verb 喜欢 (xǐhuan) instead of using 是 (shì). Both ways are possible.

A: 我喜欢看书。

Wǒ xǐhuan kàn shū.

I like to read.

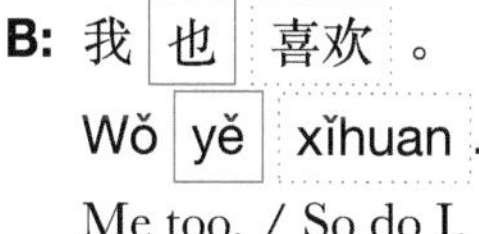

B: 我 也 喜欢 。

Wǒ yě xǐhuan .

Me too. / So do I.

You'll notice that some of those English translations use "so do I." The Chinese works exactly the same; they're just translated that way to produce more natural-sounding English.

Similar to

- Simple "noun + adjective" sentences (HSK1), page 126
- Expressing "and also" with "hai" (HSK2)

Asking about degree with “duo”

How big? How busy? How cold? Ask questions like these regarding the degree of an adjective with 多 (duō). This is just one of the many uses of this word.

Structure

多 (duō) is often used to ask about the degree or extent of something.

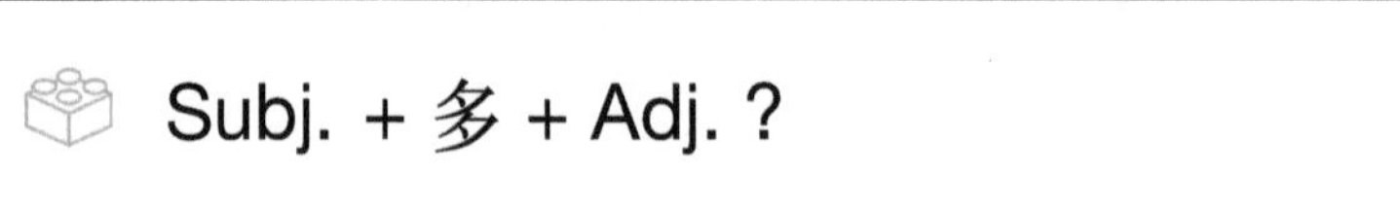

This is an easy way to ask “How [adjective] is [subject]?”

Examples

- 她 多 高?
  Tā duō gāo?
  How tall is she?
- 你家 多 大?
  Nǐ jiā duō dà?
  How large is your house?
- 你的孩子 多 大?
  Nǐ de háizi duō dà?
  How old is your child?
- 黄河 多 长?
  Huánghé duō cháng?
  How long is the Yellow River?
- 你家离这儿 多 远?
  Nǐ jiā lí zhèr duō yuǎn?
  How far is your house away from here?
- 你要在美国待 多 久?
  Nǐ yào zài Měiguó dāi duō jiǔ?
  How long are you going to stay in the USA?

- 这些东西 多 重?
  Zhèxiē dōngxi duō zhòng?
  How heavy are these things?
- 你知道我们现在 多 胖吗?
  Nǐ zhīdào wǒmen xiànzài duō pàng ma?
  Do you know how fat we are now?
- 你知道这里的冬天 多 冷吗?
  Nǐ zhīdào zhèlǐ de dōngtiān duō lěng ma?
  Do you know how cold it is here in winter?
- 你知道上海的房子 多 贵吗?
  Nǐ zhīdào Shànghǎi de fángzi duō guì ma?
  Do you know how expensive housing is in Shanghai?

大 (dà) and 小 (xiǎo) can also be used to describe ages. The question phrase 多大 (duō dà) is often used to ask "how old." However, it is an informal way to ask, usually reserved for peers, close friends, or children. The phrase 几岁 (jǐ suì) is most often used for children young enough to display their ages on one hand. Adults do not normally directly ask each other's ages in a formal setting.

Similar to

- Indicating a number in excess (HSK2)
- Intensifying with "duo" (HSK3)
- Doing something more with "duo" (HSK4)

Expressing "not very" with "bu tai"

You may be familiar with using 太 (tài) to express "too,"[1] such as when something is "too expensive" or "too hot." 不太 (bù tài) is a similar pattern for the negative, which just means "not very" or "not so" (literally "not too"). Note that this pattern does not normally use 了 (le).

不太 (bù tài) with Adjectives

Structure

Note: This pattern can also be used with non-adjectives. See below for more info.

Examples

- 我家 不太 大。
  Wǒ jiā bù tài dà.
  My house is not too big.
- 那个地方 不太 远。
  Nàge dìfang bù tài yuǎn.
  That place is not very far away.
- 老板今天 不太 高兴。
  Lǎobǎn jīntiān bù tài gāoxìng.
  The boss is not very happy today.
- 这个店的衣服 不太 贵。
  Zhège diàn de yīfu bù tài guì.
  The clothes in this shop are not too expensive.
- 我觉得他 不太 聪明。
  Wǒ juéde tā bù tài cōngming.
  I think he is not too smart.

---

1. Expressing "excessively" with "tai" (Grammar), page 124

不太 (bù tài) with Verbs

Structure

This pattern can be used with some psychological verbs (e.g. 喜欢 (xǐhuan), 想 (xiǎng), 明白 (míngbai)), as is the case with the next examples. These verbs are relatively limited.

Subj. + 不太 + Verb

Examples

- 我 不太 懂。
  Wǒ bù tài dǒng.
  I don't really understand.
- 我 不太 会说英语。
  Wǒ bù tài huì shuō Yīngyǔ.
  I can't really speak English.
- 他们 不太 想去。
  Tāmen bù tài xiǎng qù.
  They don't really want to go.
- 我哥哥 不太 喜欢他的工作。
  Wǒ gēge bù tài xǐhuan tā de gōngzuò.
  My older brother doesn't really like his job.
- 他 不太 明白老板的意思。
  Tā bù tài míngbai lǎobǎn de yìsi.
  He didn't really understand what the boss meant.

Similar to

- Expressing “excessively” with “tai” (HSK1), page 124

Expressing "and" with "he"

When listing out multiple nouns, 和 (hé) is there to help you out. Just remember that 和 (hé) isn't a word you can use to translate just *any* usage of the English word "and."

Structure

The most common way to express "and" in Chinese is with 和 (hé). It's important to note that 和 (hé) **is mainly used to link nouns**. This is how you should use it *exclusively* as you get used to it. Don't try to link verbs (or whole sentences) with 和 (hé).

Examples

- 你 和 我
  nǐ hé wǒ
  you and I
- 老板喜欢 咖啡 和 茶 。
  Lǎobǎn xǐhuan kāfēi hé chá .
  The boss likes coffee and tea.
- 我的爷爷 和 奶奶 都 70 岁。
  Wǒ de yéye hé nǎinai dōu qīshí suì.
  My grandpa and grandma are both 70 years old.
- 他 和 他女朋友 都喜欢中国菜。
  Tā hé tā nǚpéngyou dōu xǐhuan Zhōngguó cài.
  He and his girlfriend both like Chinese food.
- 你爸爸 和 你妈妈 都是美国人吗?
  Nǐ bàba hé nǐ māma dōu shì Měiguó rén ma?
  Are your father and your mother both Americans?
- 手机 和 电脑 都很贵。
  Shǒujī hé diànnǎo dōu hěn guì.
  Cell phones and computers are both expensive.

- 德语 和 法语 都很难吗?
  Déyǔ hé Fǎyǔ dōu hěn nán ma?
  Are both German and French difficult?
- 今天 和 明天 都可以吗?
  Jīntiān hé míngtiān dōu kěyǐ ma?
  Are today and tomorrow both OK?

(If you're unclear why the 都 (dōu) is used in the sentences above, see our article on the adverb 都 (dōu)[1].)

Just to be absolutely clear what we mean by using 和 (hé) with nouns only, here are two English examples of what you should and shouldn't try to express with 和 (hé):

⚠ I went to the store and bought some gum.

✔ I like to eat cucumbers and cheese.

Similar to

- Combining verbs with "bing" (HSK4)
- Expressing "and" with "he" (advanced) (HSK5)
- Expressing "as well as" with "yiji" (HSK6)

---

1. The "all" adverb "dou" (Grammar), page 21

After a specific time with “yihou”

Just as 以前 (yǐqián) can be used[1] to describe the events *before* a specific time, 以后 (yǐhòu) can be used to describe the events *after* a specific time.

Structure

This grammar structure is similar to the English “after such-and-such, something happens.” It's quite simple, all you have to do is put the “after” after the time words or time phrase.

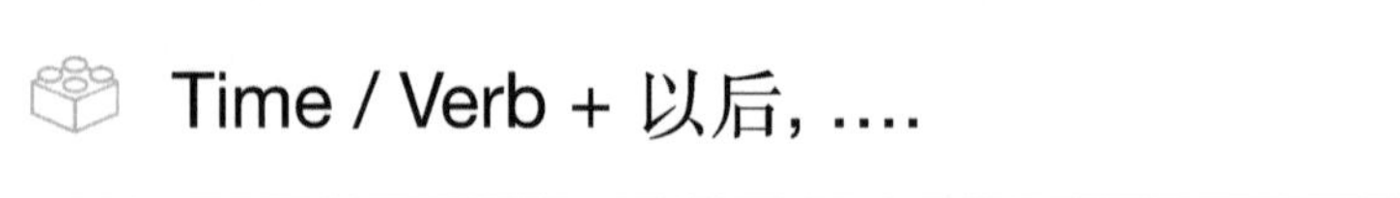

Time / Verb + 以后, ...

The time can be a time or date, or an action or event. It may or may not be in the future.

Examples

- 下午三点 以后 ，我不在家。
  Xiàwǔ sāndiǎn yǐhòu, wǒ bù zài jiā.
  After three p.m., I will not be at home.
  This one is good! “Cucumbers” and “cheese” are both nouns, so you can use 和 (hé) here.
- 来中国 以后 ，她认识了她的老公。
  Lái Zhōngguó yǐhòu, tā rènshi le tā de lǎogōng.
  After coming to China, she met her husband.
- 她 一个月 以后 开始上班。
  Tā yī gè yuè yǐhòu kāishǐ shàngbān.
  After one month, she will start working.
- 吃完午饭 以后 ，我们要开会。
  Chī wán wǔfàn yǐhòu, wǒmen yào kāihuì.
  We are going to have a meeting after we finish lunch.
- 几年 以后 ，我们公司会更大。
  Jǐ nián yǐhòu, wǒmen gōngsī huì gèng dà.
  In a few years, our company will be even bigger.

1. Before a specific time with “yiqian” (Grammar), page 36

- 老板 半个小时 以后 回来。
  Lǎobǎn bàn gè xiǎoshí yǐhòu huílái.
  After half an hour, the boss will return.
- 下班 以后 你想跟我们一起去打球吗?
  Xiàbān yǐhòu, nǐ xiǎng gēn wǒmen yīqǐ qù dǎqiú ma?
  After we get off work, would you like to go play ball with us?
- 老板 来 了 以后，大家都不说话了。
  Lǎobǎn lái le yǐhòu, dàjiā dōu bù shuōhuà le.
  After the boss came, everyone stopped talking.
- 你 到家 以后 给我打电话。
  Nǐ dào jiā yǐhòu gěi wǒ dǎ diànhuà.
  After you get home, call me.
- 结婚 以后 爸爸不喝酒了。
  Jiéhūn yǐhòu bàba bù hējiǔ le.
  After he got married, dad stopped drinking.

Note that this use of 以后 (yǐhòu) is often shortened to 后 (hòu).

Similar to

- Before a specific time with "yiqian" (HSK1, HSK3), page 36
- In the future in general with "yihou" (HSK3)
- Comparing "yihou" and "de shihou" (HSK4)
- Comparing "yihou" "ranhou" "houlai" (HSK5)
- Comparing "yihou" and "zhihou" (HSK5)

Before a specific time with "yiqian"

As well as talking about the past in general, you can use 以前 (yǐqián) to talk about things that happened *before* a specific time.

Structure

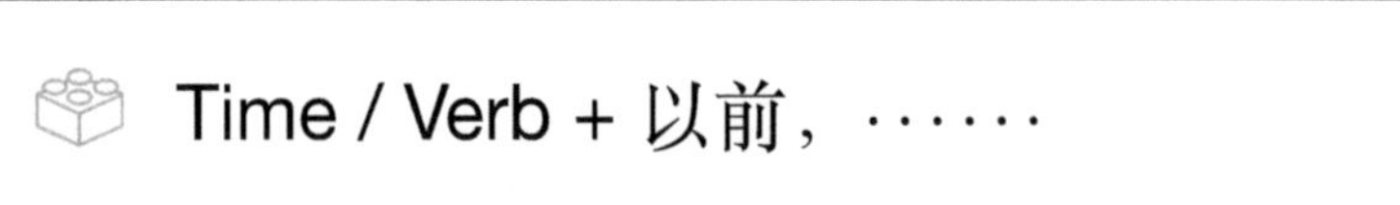

The time can be a specific time, or an action (technically, "*when* the action was done").

Examples

- 吃饭 以前，你洗手了吗?
  Chīfàn yǐqián, nǐ xǐ shǒu le ma?
  Did you wash your hands before eating?
- 睡觉 以前，不要吃东西。
  Shuìjiào yǐqián, bùyào chī dōngxi.
  Don't eat anything before you go to sleep.
- 两年 以前，你认识他吗?
  Liǎng nián yǐqián, nǐ rènshi tā ma?
  Did you know him two years ago?
- 星期五 以前，你要做完这些工作。
  Xīngqīwǔ yǐqián, nǐ yào zuò wán zhèxiē gōngzuò.
  You need to finish this work before Friday.
- 上大学 以前，你来过上海吗?
  Shàng dàxué yǐqián, nǐ lái guo shànghǎi ma?
  Before you went to college, did you ever come to Shanghai?
- 结婚 以前，你应该先买房子。
  Jiéhūn yǐqián, nǐ yīnggāi xiān mǎi fángzi.
  Before getting married, you should first buy a house.

- 二十年 以前 ，这里是一个公园。
  Èrshí nián yǐqián, zhèlǐ shì yī gè gōngyuán.
  Twenty years ago, this was a park.
- 几个月 以前 ，他们分手了。
  Jǐ gè yuè yǐqián, tāmen fēnshǒu le.
  They broke up a few months ago.
- 毕业 以前 ，我要找到工作。
  Bìyè yǐqián, wǒ yào zhǎodào gōngzuò.
  I need to find a job before graduation.
- 当总统 以前 ，Obama 没有白头发。
  Dāng zǒngtǒng yǐqián, Obama méiyǒu bái tóufa.
  Before he became the president, Obama didn't have white hair.

Note that this use of 以前 (yǐqián) can also be shortened to 前 (qián).

Similar to

- Structure of times (advanced) (HSK1, HSK3), page 56
- Structure of times (basic) (HSK1, HSK3), page 60
- Expressing "when" with "de shihou" (HSK2)
- Expressing "before" in general with "yiqian" (HSK3)
- Expressing "when" with "shi" (HSK3)
- Expressing "once" with "cengjing" (HSK5)

Time words and word order

Remembering where to put the time words, such as "yesterday," "tomorrow," "this week," etc. in a sentence is really important in order to speak Chinese correctly. In Chinese you get two equally correct choices.

Structure

Time words can appear in one of two positions in the sentence in Chinese: either at the beginning of the sentence (before the subject), or directly after the subject. The structures are:

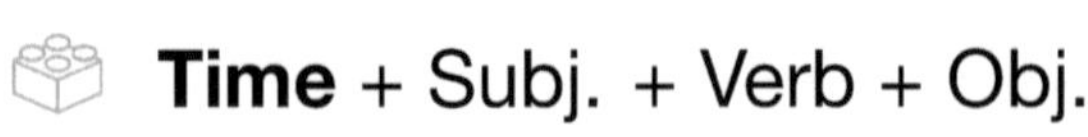

Subj. + **Time** + Verb + Obj.

So if you start speaking with "time first" English word order, you can carry on and get away with it. If, however, you're saving the time word for the *end* of the sentence, you can be pretty sure that it doesn't sound at all natural to your Chinese audience.

Examples

- 昨天 我 去了酒吧。
Zuótiān wǒ qù le jiǔbā.
Yesterday I went to the bar.
- 我 昨天 去了酒吧。
Wǒ zuótiān qù le jiǔbā.
I went to the bar yesterday.
- 下个星期 他 要回国。
Xià gè xīngqī tā yào huí guó.
Next week he is going back to his country.
- 他 下个星期 要回国。
Tā xià gè xīngqī yào huí guó.
He is going back to his country next week.

- 明年 我 要开一个公司。
  Míngnián wǒ yào kāi yī gè gōngsī.
  Next year I want to open a company.
- 我 明年 要开一个公司。
  Wǒ míngnián yào kāi yī gè gōngsī.
  I want to open a company next year.
- 下个月 我们 结婚吧?
  Xià gè yuè wǒmen jiéhūn ba?
  Next month shall we get married?
- 我们 下个月 结婚吧?
  Wǒmen xià gè yuè jiéhūn ba?
  Shall we get married next month?
- 现在 你 能来我办公室吗?
  Xiànzài nǐ néng lái wǒ bàngōngshì ma?
  Now you can come to my office?
- 你 现在 能来我办公室吗?
  Nǐ xiànzài néng lái wǒ bàngōngshì ma?
  Can you come to my office now?

Similar to

- Basic sentence order (HSK1), page 118
- Wanting to do something with “yao” (HSK2)

Age with "sui"

Use 岁 (suì) to give a person's age, similar to how we say "years old" in English. There are a details that work differently from English, however.

Basic Structure for 岁 (suì)

Structure

The structure for telling someone's age with 岁 (suì) is:

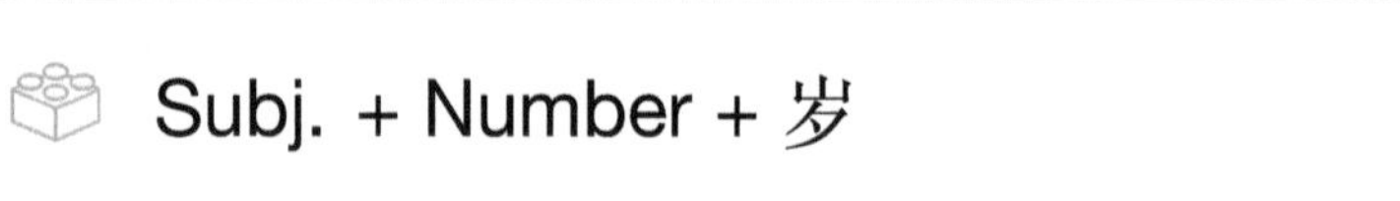

This is equivalent to someone "**is** x years old" in English. Notice that you don't need to include any verb when you use 岁 (suì).

Examples

- 我 20 岁 。
  Wǒ èrshí suì.
  I am 20 years old.
- 我儿子一 岁 。
  Wǒ érzi yī suì.
  My son is one year old.
- 我妈妈今年 45 岁 。
  Wǒ māma jīnnián sìshí-wǔ suì.
  My mother is 45 years old this year.
- 你爷爷今年 80 岁 吗?
  Nǐ yéye jīnnián bāshí suì ma?
  Is your grandpa eighty years old this year?
- 他女朋友也 20 岁 吗?
  Tā nǚpéngyou yě èrshí suì ma?
  Is his girlfriend also twenty years old?

Note that you shouldn't use either the verb 是 (shì) or the measure word like 个 (gè) in any of these sentences.

- ✘ 我的孩子一 个 岁 。
  Wǒ de háizi yī gè suì.

✗ 我的孩子 是 一 岁 。

Wǒ de háizi shì yī suì.

✓ 我的孩子一 岁 。

Wǒ de háizi yī suì.

My child is one year old.

Adding "And a Half" to an Age

Structure

The word for "half" in Chinese is 半 (bàn), and you simply add this after 岁 (suì).

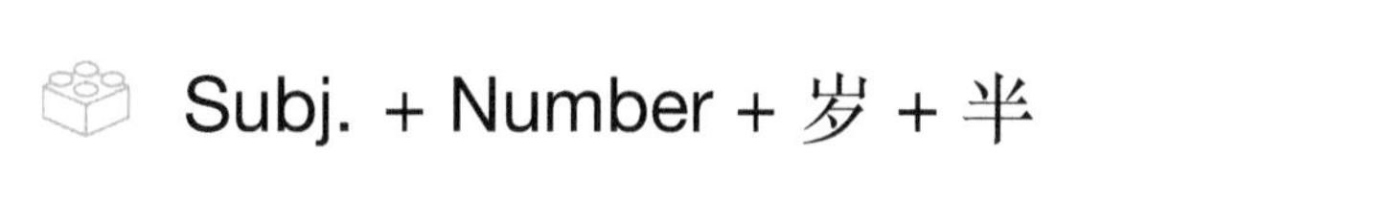

Subj. + Number + 岁 + 半

Examples

- 她两岁半。

  Tā liǎng suì bàn.

  She is two and a half years old.

- 我儿子一 岁 半。

  Wǒ érzi yī suì bàn.

  My son is one and a half years old.

Similar to

- Measure word "ge" (HSK1), page 42

Measure word "ge"

个 (gè) is the most commonly used measure word. It can be used in a pinch for any noun if you can't think of a more precise measure word. (Although you might not sound quite as smart, you'll still get your point across). Also, for many nouns, 个 (gè) *is* the only correct measure word.

Counting Nouns

Structure

The general structure for 个 (gè) and measure words in general is:

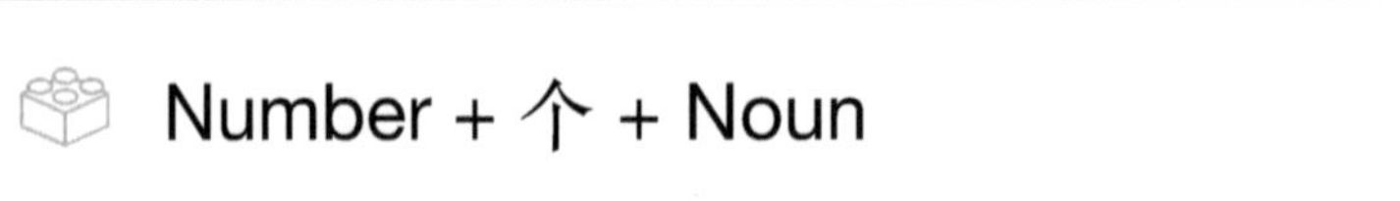

Any time you want to state *how many* of a noun in Chinese, you probably need a measure word. First get used to how they are used with 个 (gè).

Examples

- 一 个 人
  yī gè rén
  one person
- 四 个 朋友
  sì gè péngyou
  four friends
- 三 个 苹果手机
  sān gè Píngguǒ shǒujī
  three iPhones
- 五 个 星期
  wǔ gè xīngqī
  five weeks
- 六 个 月
  liù gè yuè
  six months
- 两 个 老婆
  liǎng gè lǎopo
  two wives

- 十 个 男人，七 个 傻，八 个 坏。 *A line from a song*
  Shí gè nánrén, qī gè shǎ, bā gè huài.
  Ten men: seven are fools, and eight are bad.

Omitting the Number

Structure

If the number is one (1), you can omit it and use 个 (gè) by itself. This is similar to "a" or "an" in English, for example in "a person" or "an idiot." (The tone on 个 (gè) is normally somewhat de-emphasized in this usage, but still written as fourth tone. You don't need to stress about it, though.)

Examples

- 他是 个 老外。
  Tā shì gè lǎowài.
  He is a foreigner.
- 我有 个 儿子。
  Wǒ yǒu gè érzi.
  I have a son.
- 她是 个 好老师。
  Tā shì gè hǎo lǎoshī.
  She is a good teacher.
- 你想吃 个 包子吗?
  Nǐ xiǎng chī gè bāozi ma?
  Would you like to eat a stuffed steamed bun?
- 老师，我有 个 问题。
  Lǎoshī, wǒ yǒu gè wèntí.
  Teacher, I have a question.

Similar to

- Age with "sui" (HSK1), page 40
- Measure words in quantity questions (HSK1), page 134

- Measure words for counting (HSK2)
- Measure words with “this” and “that” (HSK2)
- Ordinal numbers with “di” (HSK2)

Structure of dates

Dates in Chinese follow the order "year, month, day." This is in keeping with the "from big to small" trend which pervades many facets of Chinese culture.

Structure

Dates are arranged from largest unit to smallest: *year, month, day*.

x 年 + y 月 + z 日

So April 1st, 2019 is **2019 年 4 月 1 日** (**èr-líng-yī-jiǔ** nián **Sì**yuè **yī** rì).

Note that 号 (hào) is commonly used in *spoken* Mandarin instead of 日 (rì):

x 年 + y 月 + z 号

The above example becomes: **2019 年 4 月 1 号** (**èr-líng-yī-jiǔ** nián **Sì**yuè **yī** hào). In written Chinese, however, you will see 日 (rì) rather than 号 (hào).

Examples

- 1868 年 1 月 18 号
  Yī-bā-liù-bā nián Yī yuè shíbā hào
  January 18, 1868
- 1910 年 8 月 9 号
  Yī-jiǔ-yī-líng nián Bā yuè jiǔ hào
  August 9, 1910
- 2001 年 7 月 20 日
  èr-líng-líng-yī nián Qī yuè èrshí rì
  July 20th, 2001
- 1 月 1 日 是新年。
  Yī yuè yī rì shì Xīnnián.
  January 1st is New Year's Day.

- 12 月 24 日 是平安夜。
  Shí-èr yuè èrshí-sì rì shì Píng'ān Yè.
  December 24th is Christmas Eve.
- 10 月 1 号 我们去上海。
  Shí yuè yī hào wǒmen qù Shànghǎi.
  We will go to Shanghai on October 1st.
- 我 1990 年 7 月 出生。
  Wǒ Yī-jiǔ-jiǔ-líng nián Qī yuè chūshēng.
  I was born in July 1990.
- 你的生日是 11 月 11 号 吗?
  Nǐ de shēngrì shì Shíyī yuè shíyī hào ma?
  Is your birthday November 11th?
- 我 2006 年 4 月 17 号 认识了他。
  Wǒ èr-líng-líng-liù nián Sì yuè shíqī hào rènshi le tā.
  I met him on April 17, 2006.
- 1980 年 9 月 4 号 我们结婚了。
  Yī-jiǔ-bā-líng nián Jiǔ yuè sì hào wǒmen jiéhūn le.
  We got married on September 4th, 1980.

Similar to

- Structure of days of the week (HSK1), page 47
- Structure of numbers (HSK1), page 50
- Structure of times (advanced) (HSK1, HSK3), page 56
- Structure of times (basic) (HSK1, HSK3), page 60

Structure of days of the week

星期 (xīngqī) means "week" in Chinese. This is also used to indicate which weekday you are talking about.

Structure

Days of the week in Chinese are formed by the word "week" followed by a number:

English	Chinese
Monday	星期一 Xīngqīyī
Tuesday	星期二 Xīngqī'èr
Wednesday	星期三 Xīngqīsān
Thursday	星期四 Xīngqīsì
Friday	星期五 Xīngqīwǔ
Saturday	星期六 Xīngqīliù
Sunday	星期天 Xīngqītiān

Notice that Sunday is the only exception. Rather than a number, 天 (tiān) is used. More formally, Sunday is also referred to as 星期日 (Xīngqīrì).

One other implication of this system that you may not have noticed: "day one" is Monday. In Chinese culture, the first day of the week is Monday, and *not* Sunday.

Examples

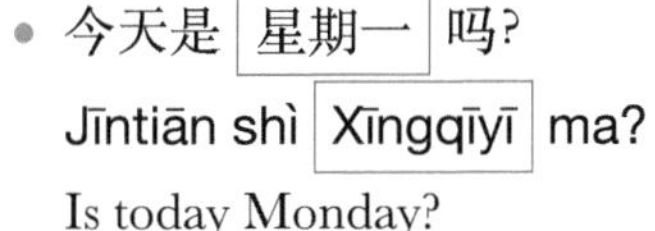

- 今天是 星期一 吗?
  Jīntiān shì Xīngqīyī ma?
  Is today Monday?

是 is optional

- 明天 星期五 ，太高兴了。 *Optional 是 omitted*
  Míngtiān Xīngqīwǔ, tài gāoxìng le.
  Tomorrow is Friday. I'm so happy.
- 星期三 我不在上海。
  Xīngqīsān wǒ bù zài Shànghǎi.
  I'm not here in Shanghai on Wednesday.
- 星期二 早上我很忙。
  Xīngqī'èr zǎoshang wǒ hěn máng.
  I am busy on Tuesday morning.
- 你 星期天 要做什么？
  Nǐ Xīngqītiān yào zuò shénme?
  What are you doing on Sunday?
- 上个 星期五 我跟他见面了。
  Shàng gè Xīngqīwǔ wǒ gēn tā jiànmiàn le.
  I met him last Friday.
- 这个 星期三 晚上你有空吗？
  Zhège Xīngqīsān wǎnshang nǐ yǒu kòng ma?
  Are you free this Wednesday evening?
- 下个 星期四 是我的生日。
  Xià gè Xīngqīsì shì wǒ de shēngrì.
  My birthday is on next Thursday.
- 这个 星期五 晚上我们要去酒吧。
  Zhège Xīngqīwǔ wǎnshang wǒmen yào qù jiǔbā.
  We're going to a bar this Friday night.
- 星期六 和 星期天 我们不上班。
  Xīngqīliù hé Xīngqītiān wǒmen bù shàngbān.
  Saturday and Sunday we don't work.

Other Words for "Week"

Hopefully this doesn't freak you out, but there are actually two other ways to say "week" in Chinese. You should still learn 星期 (xīngqī) first, and that's really all you need as a beginner.

The other words for "week" are 礼拜 (lǐbài) and 周 (zhōu). Skip them for now unless you really need them.

Similar to

- Structure of dates (HSK1), page 45
- Structure of numbers (HSK1), page 50
- Structure of times (advanced) (HSK1, HSK3), page 56
- Structure of times (basic) (HSK1, HSK3), page 60

Structure of numbers

Chinese handles numbers in a very consistent and logical way. Once you've mastered just a few tricky parts, you will know how to read out any number in Chinese.

One to One Hundred

Structure for the First Ten

You just have to memorize these ten; nothing tricky there.

Numeral	Character	Pinyin
1	一	yī
2	二	èr
3	三	sān
4	四	sì
5	五	wǔ
6	六	liù
7	七	qī
8	八	bā
9	九	jiǔ
10	十	shí

Phone Numbers

Like in American English, Chinese phone numbers are given as a string of individual numbers, using the digits 0-9. The only trick is that the number 1 is often pronounced "yāo" instead of "yī" to avoid confusion with number 7, which is pronounced "qī."

- 110 *Number for the police in the PRC*

  yāo yāo líng

- 120 *Number for an ambulance in the PRC*

  yāo èr líng

- 119 *Number to report a fire in the PRC*

  yāo yāo jiǔ

- 13501200120 *Cell phone numbers are 11 digits in the PRC*

  yāo sān wǔ, líng yāo èr líng, líng yāo èr líng

Structure for Teens

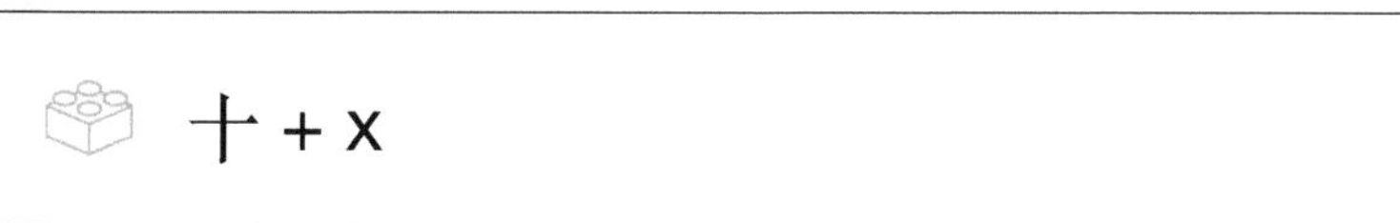

Eleven, twelve and the teens are handled very logically. They're formed with 十 (shí) followed by a digit 一 (yī) to 九 (jiǔ). So eleven is 十一 (shíyī), twelve is 十二 (shí'èr), thirteen is 十三 (shísān), and so on up to nineteen, which is 十九 (shíjiǔ).

Numeral	Character	Pinyin
11	十一	shíyī
12	十二	shí'èr
13	十三	shísān
14	十四	shísì
15	十五	shíwǔ
16	十六	shíliù
17	十七	shíqī
18	十八	shíbā
19	十九	shíjiǔ

Structure for Tens

All the tens are also formed very logically. Twenty is 二十 (èrshí), thirty is 三十 (sānshí), and so on. Units in the tens are simply added on the end. So twenty one is 二十一 (èrshí-yī), thirty four is 三十四 (sānshí-sì), and ninety-nine is 九十九 (jiǔshí-jiǔ). All very logical and consistent.

x + 十 + y

Examples

Numeral	Character	Pinyin
20	二十	èrshí
23	二十三	èrshí-sān
30	三十	sānshí
39	三十九	sānshí-jiǔ
40	四十	sìshí
44	四十四	sìshí-sì
50	五十	wǔshí
73	七十三	qīshí-sān
82	八十二	bāshí-èr
97	九十七	jiǔshí-qī

And one hundred is simply 一百 (yībǎi), as in English. So you now know how to count to one hundred in Chinese.

After One Hundred

Dealing with Zeroes

Note: when there's a "0" in the middle of a number, you read it as 零 (líng), and don't put a unit (like "ten" or "hundred") after it. In the following examples, we'll show what happens when the "tens" place is a zero in a three-digit number.

Structure

x + 百 + 零 + y

Examples

Numeral	Character	Pinyin
101	一百零一	yībǎi líng yī
202	二百零二	èrbǎi líng èr
206	二百零六	èrbǎi líng liù
305	三百零五	sānbǎi líng wǔ
407	四百零七	sìbǎi líng qī
504	五百零四	wǔbǎi líng sì
602	六百零二	liùbǎi líng èr
701	七百零一	qībǎi líng yī
803	八百零三	bābǎi líng sān
909	九百零九	jiǔbǎi líng jiǔ

For Numbers 110 and Greater

For numbers greater than 100, if the number ends in zero (110, 230, 370, 450, etc.), a number like 150 can be read as 一百五十 (yībǎi wǔshí), but is often read as 一百五 (yībǎi wǔ). In fact, reading it as 一百五 (yībǎi wǔ) *always* means 150, never 105. As described above, 105 would be read as 一百零五 (yībǎi líng wǔ).

For numbers greater than 100 that end in a number in the teens, it's normal to pronounce the ten as "yīshí" rather than just "shí" (see the examples below).

Also, sometimes the number "200" is read as 二百 (èrbǎi), but often it is read as 两百 (liǎngbǎi). Both are OK. (This is an 二 (èr) vs. 两 (liǎng) issue which you may or may not have encountered before.)

Structure

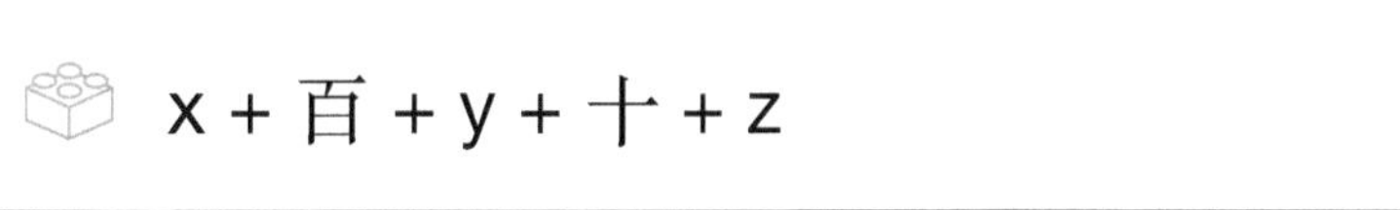

Examples

Numeral	Character	Pinyin
110	一百一十	yībǎi yīshí
111	一百一十一	yībǎi yīshí-yī
210	二百一十	èrbǎi yīshí
350	三百五十	sānbǎi wǔshí
480	四百八十	sìbǎi bāshí
550	五百五十	wǔbǎi wǔshí
635	六百三十五	liùbǎi sānshí-wǔ
777	七百七十七	qībǎi qīshí-qī
832	八百三十二	bābǎi sānshí-èr
999	九百九十九	jiǔbǎi jiǔshí-jiǔ

After One Thousand

千 (qiān) means "thousand" in Chinese. Its rules of usage are similar to the rules for "hundred." Just note that no matter how many zeroes are in the middle of the number, you just say 零 (líng) once.

Examples

Numeral	Character	Pinyin
1001	一千零一	yīqiān líng yī
1010	一千零一十	yīqiān líng yīshí
1019	一千零一十九	yīqiān líng yīshí-jiǔ
1020	一千零二十	yīqiān líng èrshí
1100	一千一百	yīqiān yībǎi
1101	一千一百零一	yīqiān yībǎi líng yī
1234	一千二百三十四	yīqiān èrbǎi sānshí-sì
2345	两千三百四十五	liǎngqiān sānbǎi sìshí-wǔ

8765	八千七百六十五	bāqiān qībǎi liùshí-wǔ
9999	九千九百九十九	jiǔqiān jiǔbǎi jiǔshí-jiǔ

10,000 and beyond

Things get a little trickier once you get to 10,000. If you're ready for it, you can move on to big numbers.

Similar to

- Structure of dates (HSK1), page 45
- Structure of days of the week (HSK1), page 47
- Structure of times (advanced) (HSK1, HSK3), page 56
- Structure of times (basic) (HSK1, HSK3), page 60
- Comparing "er" and "liang" (HSK2)
- Approximating with sequential numbers (HSK3)

Structure of times (advanced)

If you already know the basics of how to tell time in Chinese[1], you may want to get a little more specific or sophisticated, using words like 分 (fēn) and 刻 (kè).

Minutes Past the Hour

Minutes are marked with 分 (fēn) (short for 分钟 (fēnzhōng)). The way to include them in the time depends on whether they're minutes *past* or *to* the hour.

Minutes *past* the hour are expressed after 点 (diǎn) in the same way as half and quarter hours.

Minutes Less Than 10

Structure

In Chinese, when the minute is under 10, the word 零 (líng) is often used after 点 (diǎn). For example, 2:07 would be said as "两点零七分" (liǎng diǎn líng qī fēn). However, note that when speaking, it is very common for most Chinese people take out the "分 (fēn)" at the end of the time.

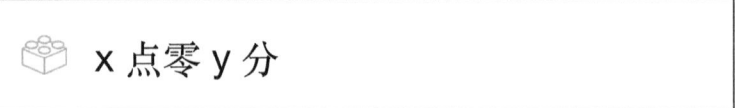

x 点零 y 分

Examples

- 两 点 零 九 分
  liǎng diǎn líng jiǔ fēn
  2:09
- 三 点 零 八 分
  sān diǎn líng bā fēn
  3:08
- 五 点 零 三 分
  wǔ diǎn líng sān fēn
  5:03

1. Structure of times (basic) (Grammar), page 60

- 七 点 零 一 分
  qī diǎn líng yī fēn
  7:01
- 八 点 零 五 分
  bā diǎn líng wǔ fēn
  8:05

Minutes Greater Than 10

There's nothing tricky about this, since there's no 零 (líng). Just remember that in casual speech, the 分 (fēn) at the end is sometimes dropped.

Structure

Examples

- 一 点 四十 分
  yī diǎn sìshí fēn
  1:40
- 两 点 十 分
  liǎng diǎn shí fēn
  2:10
- 三 点 二十 分
  sān diǎn èrshí fēn
  3:20
- 七 点 十五 分
  qī diǎn shíwǔ fēn
  7:15
- 九 点 五十 分
  jiǔ diǎn wǔshí fēn
  9:50

Quarter Hours

In Chinese, quarter hours are only expressed on the 1st quarter x:15, and the third quarter x:45. Like half hours, they also come after the word 点 (diǎn). We use the word 刻 (kè) to express "quarter hour."

Structure

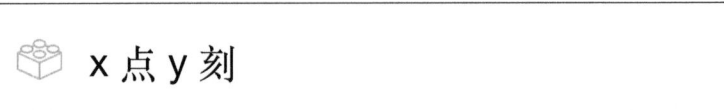

Examples

- 九 点 一 刻
  jiǔ diǎn yī kè
  9:15
- 十二 点 一 刻
  shí'èr diǎn yī kè
  12:15
- 六 点 三 刻
  liù diǎn sān kè
  6:45

You can totally just use 十五分 (shíwǔ fēn) for "15 minutes (past)" or 四十五分 (sìshí-wǔ fēn) for "45 minutes (past)" if you're lazy, though. It also works!

Minutes to the Hour

When expressing how many minutes it will be till the next full hour, you put 差 (chā) in front of the time expression.

Structure

Minutes *to* the hour use this structure:

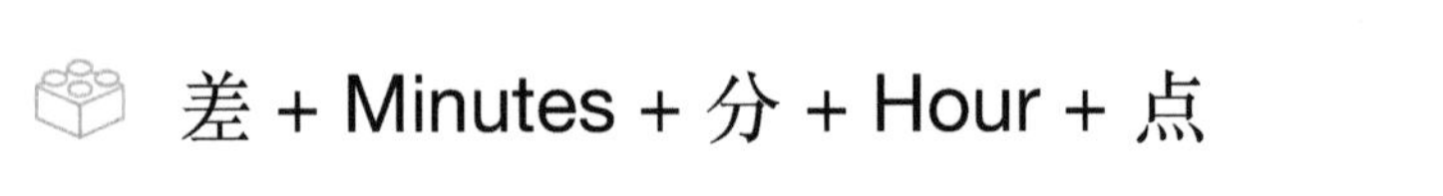

or

Hour + 点 + 差 + Minutes + 分

Examples

- 差 五分三 点
  chā wǔ fēn sān diǎn
  five minutes til 3 o'clock
- 十二 点 差 三分
  shí'èr diǎn chā sān fēn
  three minutes til 12 o'clock
- 差 五分八 点 半
  chā wǔ fēn bā diǎn bàn
  five minutes til 8:30
- 十 点 差 两分
  shí diǎn chā liǎng fēn
  two minutes til 10:00

HSK Notes

Only the basic 分 (fēn) usage is tested on HSK1. The others are not tested until HSK3.

Similar to

- Structure of times (basic) (HSK1, HSK3), page 60

Structure of times (basic)

Time in Chinese, just like in English, is expressed by stating the hour first, and then the minute (big to small).

On the Hour

The time of day in Chinese is formed with a number[1] 1 to 12 (一 (yī) to 十二 (shí'èr)) followed by 点 (diǎn). This 点 (diǎn) is equivalent to *o'clock* in English. In China, people generally use a twelve-hour clock, preceded by 上午 (shàngwǔ) for "a.m." or 下午 (xiàwǔ) for "p.m." when necessary.

Structure

 (Date and/or time of day +) x 点

Sometimes people use the longer 点钟 (diǎnzhōng) instead of just 点 (diǎn), but you're fine using the short form.

Examples

If you want to include more specific information, start with the day or date, followed by the general time of day, with the exact clock time last. (This is the big-to-small pattern.) This is how Chinese gets around the need for "a.m." or "p.m.": use 上午 (shàngwǔ) for times in the morning, and 下午 (xiàwǔ) for times in the afternoon.

- 九 点
  jiǔ diǎn
  9 o'clock
- 上午七 点
  shàngwǔ qī diǎn
  7 o'clock a.m.
- 下午四 点
  xiàwǔ sì diǎn
  4 o'clock p.m.
- 中午十二 点
  zhōngwǔ shí'èr diǎn
  12 o'clock noon

---

1. Structure of numbers (Grammar), page 50

- 明天晚上七 点
  míngtiān wǎnshang qī diǎn
  7 o'clock p.m. tomorrow evening
- 9 月 9 号早上六 点
  jiǔ yuè jiǔ hào zǎoshang liù diǎn
  September 9th, 6 o'clock a.m.
- 星期三上午九 点
  Xīngqīsān shàngwǔ jiǔ diǎn
  Wednesday at 9 o'clock a.m.

Note that **two o'clock is 两点** (liǎng diǎn), not 二点 (èr diǎn). (For more information on when to use 两 (liǎng) vs. 二 (èr), see our article on comparing "er" and "liang").

"*Twelve* o'clock," however, is still 十二点 (shí'èr diǎn).

Half Hours

Half hours are added after 点 (diǎn) and are indicated with 半 (bàn).

Structure

Examples

- 五 点半
  wǔ diǎn bàn
  5:30
- 下午两 点半
  xiàwǔ liǎng diǎn bàn
  2:30 p.m.
- 星期天上午十 点半
  Xīngqītiān shàngwǔ shí diǎn bàn
  Sunday at 10:30 a.m.
- 昨天晚上七 点半
  zuótiān wǎnshang qī diǎn bàn
  7:30 yesterday evening

- 今天下午四 点半
  jīntiān xiàwǔ sì diǎn bàn
  4:30 p.m. this afternoon.

As a beginner, that should be all you need. If you've mastered all of these structures and want to get a little more advanced, see structure of times (advanced)[1].

HSK Notes

Simple times with 点 (diǎn) is on HSK1, but the usage above with 半 (bàn) is not. It is not tested until HSK3.

Similar to

- Before a specific time with "yiqian" (HSK1, HSK3), page 36
- Structure of dates (HSK1), page 45
- Structure of numbers (HSK1), page 50
- Structure of times (advanced) (HSK1, HSK3), page 56

1. Structure of times (advanced) (Grammar), page 56

Expressing "not anymore" with "le"

In a negative sentence, the sentence-final 了 (le) can take on the meaning of "(not) anymore" or "no longer." The word 已经 (yǐjīng), which means "already," may nor may not accompany it.

不 with Only 了

Structure

Examples

- 我 不 想吃 了 。
  Wǒ bù xiǎng chī le .
  I don't want to eat anymore.
- 你 不 喜欢我 了 吗?
  Nǐ bù xǐhuan wǒ le ma?
  You don't like me anymore?
- 你们 不 能打 了 。
  Nǐmen bù néng dǎ le .
  You can't fight anymore.

没有 with Only 了

Structure

Examples

- 没有 纸 了 。
  Méiyǒu zhǐ le .
  There's no paper anymore.

  in other words, "we're out of paper"

- 手机 没 电 了 。
  Shǒujī méi diàn le.
  My cell phone has run out of power.
- 他 没有 家 了 。
  Tā méiyǒu jiā le.
  He doesn't have his home anymore.

Adding 已经 for Emphasis

已经 (yǐjīng) is optional for this pattern, but either 不 (bù) or 没有 (méiyǒu) will be needed to make the verb negative. The sentence-final 了 (le) is, of course, required.

Structure

已经 + 不 + [Verb Phrase] + 了

已经 + 没 (有) + [Noun Phrase] + 了

Examples

- 我 已經 不 住这里 了 。
  Wǒ yǐjīng bù zhù zhèlǐ le.
  I don't live here anymore.
- 他 已经 不 在这儿工作 了 。
  Tā yǐjīng bù zài zhèr gōngzuò le.
  He doesn't work here anymore.
- 他们 已经 不 在一起 了 。
  Tāmen yǐjīng bù zài yīqǐ le.
  They are no longer together.

- 我们 已经 没有 钱 了 。
  Wǒmen yǐjīng méiyǒu qián le.
  We all don't have money anymore.

Expressing "now" with "le"

现在 (xiànzài) isn't the only way to express "now." You'll notice that in many common expressions, 了 (le) is used in place of the word for "now."

Structure

This pattern is actually the same as change of state with "le", but the examples below are somewhat idiomatic and can also easily be confused with a direct translation of "now" in Chinese, so they get special treatment here.

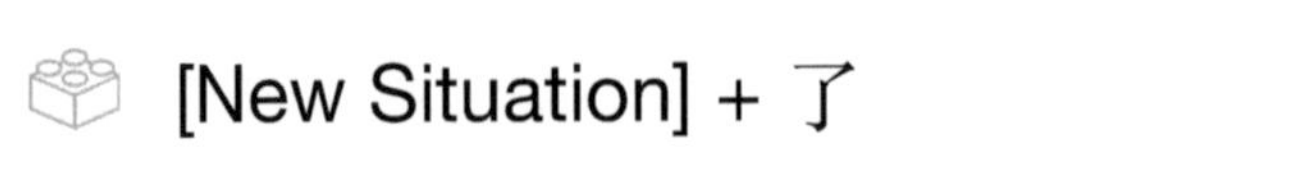

Examples

- 知道 了 。
  Zhīdào le.
  Got it. / I see.
  This is something I didn't know before now
- 懂 了 。
  Dǒng le.
  Now I understand.
- 我 20 岁 了 !
  Wǒ èrshí suì le!
  I'm 20 years old now!
- 吃饭 了 !
  Chīfàn le!
  Time to eat!
- 我走 了 。
  Wǒ zǒu le.
  I'm leaving now.
- 他来 了 。
  Tā lái le.
  He's coming over now. / He's on the way.
  This can also mean "He's here now." Be careful!

- 上课 了 ！
  Shàngkè le!
  Class begins now!
- 我去睡觉 了 。
  Wǒ qù shuìjiào le.
  I'm going to bed now.
- 快点儿，开会 了 ！
  Kuài diǎnr, kāihuì le!
  Hurry up, it's time for the meeting now!
- 到你 了 。
  Dào nǐ le.
  It's your turn now.

Expressing close possession without "de"

Expressing possession[1] in Chinese is accomplished with the particle 的 (de). But sometimes when certain (especially close) relationships are involved, it's more natural to drop the 的 (de).

Structure

 Pronoun + Noun

Normally possession[1] is expressed using the particle 的 (de). However, you can omit 的 (de) in these cases:

- A close personal relationship is involved (family, close friends, boyfriends or girlfriends)
- An institutional or organizational relationship is involved (school, work)

In these cases 的 (de) **should be** omitted. It doesn't sound as natural if you leave it in.

Examples

- 我家 很大。
  Wǒ jiā hěn dà.
  My house is very big.
- 你哥哥 很高。
  Nǐ gōgo hǒn gāo.
  Your big brother is very tall.
- 这是 我女朋友 。
  Zhè shì wǒ nǚpéngyou .
  This is my girlfriend.
- 她妈妈 很漂亮。
  Tā māma hěn piàoliang.
  Her mom is very pretty.

---

1. Expressing possession with "de" (Grammar), page 74

- 我们学校 很大。
  Wǒmen xuéxiào hěn dà.
  Our school is big.
- 他们公司 在北京。
  Tāmen gōngsī zài Běijīng.
  Their company is in Bejing.
- 你男朋友 很帅。
  Nǐ nánpéngyou hěn shuài.
  Your boyfriend is very handsome.
- 他儿子 很有名。
  Tā érzi hěn yǒumíng.
  His son is really famous.
- 我女儿 会说英语。
  Wǒ nǚ'ér huì shuō Yīngyǔ.
  My daughter can speak English.
- 他爸爸 是 我们公司 的老板。
  Tā bàba shì wǒmen gōngsī de lǎobǎn.
  His dad is the boss of our company.

If 的 (de) was used in the above examples, it would create an unnatural sense of distance between the two.

Similar to

- Expressing possession with “de” (HSK1), page 74
- Expressing possession with “you” (HSK1), page 92

Expressing completion with "le"

Also known as: 了1, verb 了, completed action 了 and perfective aspect 了.

The particle 了 (le) has a lot of uses. One of the most common is to express the completion of an action. This is called aspect, which is not the same as tense. Tense is about *when an action happens*: past, present or future. With regards to 了 (le), aspect is about *whether the action is complete* in a certain time frame.

Most Basic Pattern

The simplest way to use 了 (le) is to just put it after a verb. When there's nothing else after the verb, there are no complications!

Structure

Subj. + Verb + 了

Examples

- 他们到 了 。
  Tāmen dào le .
  They have arrived.
- 我买 了 。
  Wǒ mǎi le .
  I've bought it.
- 我们都去 了 。
  Wǒmen dōu qù le .
  We all went.
- 我找到 了 ！
  Wǒ zhǎodào le !
  I found it!

Putting 了 After a Verb with an Object

Here is where things start to get slightly more complicated. If the verb has an object, 了 (le) can go directly after the verb to indicate completion, but there are a few other conditions that should be met.

When Time is Specified

It's a good idea to specify the time[1] anyway, if you're still getting used to Chinese verbs not indicating tenses by themselves. When you do this, it's generally OK to put the 了 (le) right after the verb and before the object.

Structure

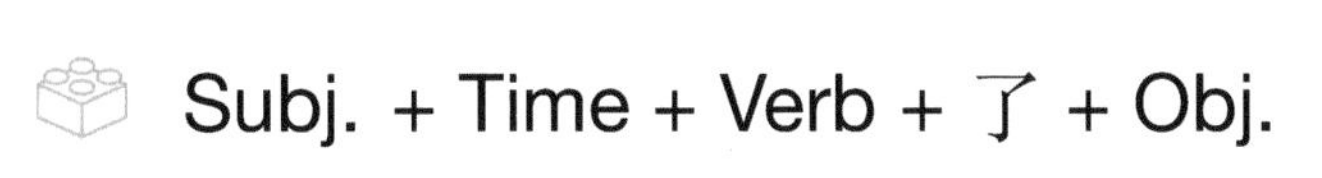
Subj. + Time + Verb + 了 + Obj.

Time + Subj. + Verb + 了 + Obj.

Examples

- 我 今天 吃 了 早饭。
  Wǒ jīntiān chī le zǎofàn.
  This morning I ate breakfast.
- 她 上个月 去 了 北京。
  Tā shàng gè yuè qù le Běijīng.
  Last month she went to Beijing.
- 中午 我见 了 朋友。
  Zhōngwǔ wǒ jiàn le péngyou.
  At noon I met a friend.

When the Object's Quantity is Specified

This pattern works if the sentence includes more information about the object, such as how many there are.

Structure

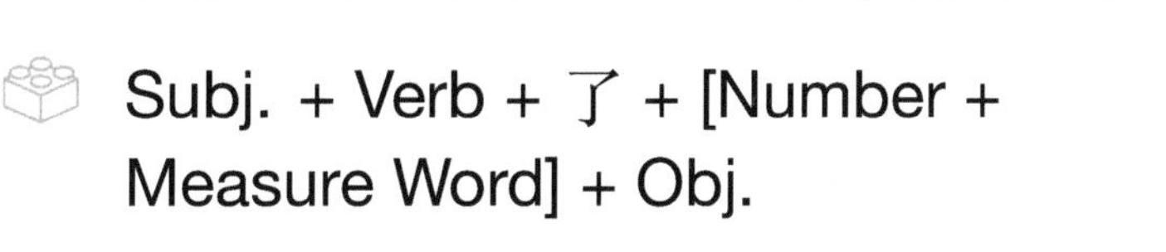
Subj. + Verb + 了 + [Number + Measure Word] + Obj.

1. Time words and word order (Grammar), page 38

(Make sure you're clear on what a measure word is and how to use them.)

Examples

- 老师问 了 五个 问题。
  Lǎoshī wèn le wǔ gè wèntí.
  The teacher asked five questions.
- 我买 了 三本 书。
  Wǒ mǎi le sān běn shū.
  I bought three books.
- 我喝 了 两杯 咖啡。
  Wǒ hē le liǎng bēi kāfēi.
  I drank two cups of coffee.

When 了 Comes After the Object

OK, so here's the tricky part. Even when indicating completion, the 了 (le) can sometimes go after the object. This is not a topic that can be covered in depth at the elementary level, but you should be aware that this does happen too.

Structure

Subj. + Verb + Obj. + 了

Examples

- 上个月我去 台湾 了 。
  Shàng gè yuè wǒ qù Táiwān le.
  I went to Taiwan last month.
- 昨天晚上我看见 UFO 了 。
  Zuótiān wǎnshang wǒ kànjiàn le UFO.
  I saw a UFO last night.

If you're upper intermediate-ish and think you can "handle the truth," also check out our more advanced, full exposé on 了 (le) after an object.

Putting 了 After Consecutive Actions

So what happens if a whole string of things happened in the past? Do you have to put a 了 (le) after each one, just like we'd put each verb in the past tense in English? Good question! The short answer is that you only need one 了 (le).

To keep things simple, we'll make the first action "coming" or "going" somewhere, which will be followed by another action. So we'll be using 来 (lái) or 去 (qù) plus a place in each sentence, and then another action. For this type of "consecutive action," 了 (le) should be placed after the *final* verb (or verb phrase), which marks the completion of the entire sequence.

Structure

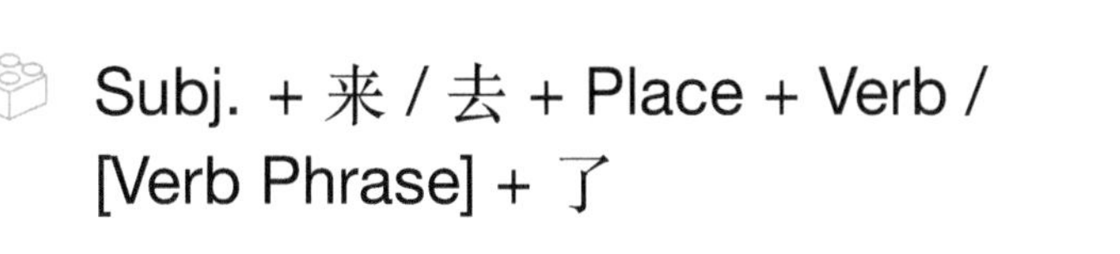
Subj. + 来 / 去 + Place + Verb / [Verb Phrase] + 了

Examples

- 昨天她 来 我家 吃饭 了 。
  Zuótiān tā lái wǒ jiā chīfàn le.
  She came to my place and ate dinner yesterday.
- 我们上周 去 北京 开会 了 。
  Wǒmen shàng zhōu qù Běijīng kāihuì le.
  We went to Beijing and had a meeting there last week.
- 我和朋友 去 商场 买衣服 了 。
  Wǒ hé péngyou qù shāngchǎng mǎi yīfu le.
  I went to the mall with my friend and bought some clothes.

Completion in the Future

了 (le) can appear in sentences about the future as well as the past. What's important is whether or not the action has been *completed*, no matter what time frame we're talking about. This also means that this 了 (le) isn't used with habitual or continuous actions.

Similar to

- Time words and word order (HSK1), page 38
- Expressing experiences with "guo" (HSK2)
- Using "guo" with "le" (HSK2)
- Advanced "le" after an object (HSK5)

Expressing possession with "de"

In Chinese, possession is marked with the particle 的 (de), placed after the "owner" noun or noun phrase. This particle works in a similar way to apostrophe-"s" in English, but is used much more broadly in Chinese. This article highlights one of its simplest and most common usages.

Structure

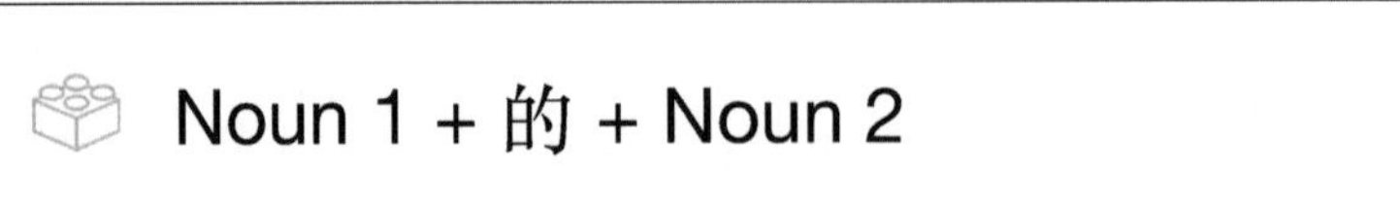

This means "**Noun 1's Noun 2**" (where Noun 2 belongs to Noun 1).

The structure is super simple. It will take a bit of time before you realize how truly universal this pattern is. It doesn't matter whether the "Noun 1" is a person, place, or thing, or even if it's a pronoun (like "he," "she," or "it"). The structure stays consistent.

Examples

- 我 的 老师
  wǒ de lǎoshī
  my teacher
- 你 的 手机
  nǐ de shǒujī
  your cell phone
- 我们 的 钱
  wǒmen de qián
  our money
- 他们 的 东西
  tāmen de dōngxi
  their stuff
- 爸爸 的 车
  bàba de chē
  dad's car

- 你们 的 菜
  nǐmen de cài
  your food
- 北京 的 空气
  Běijīng de kōngqì
  Beijing's air
- 公司 的 老板
  gōngsī de lǎobǎn
  the company's boss
- 上海 的 天气
  Shànghǎi de tiānqì
  Shanghai's weather
- 老师 的 朋友
  lǎoshī de péngyou
  teacher's friend

Similar to

- Expressing close possession without “de” (HSK1), page 68
- Expressing possession with “you” (HSK1), page 92

Questions with "ne"

The particle 呢 (ne) can be used to ask reciprocal questions, also known as "bounce back" questions. 呢 (ne) can also be used to form simple questions asking "what about...?" or "how about...?"

General Questions with 呢 (ne)

Structure

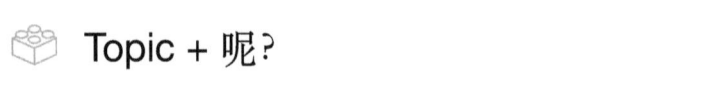

And it's as simple as that. Say what you want to ask about, then stick 呢 (ne) on the end. A very common way to use this is to return a question after being asked it. The classic example is this exchange:

A: 你好吗?

Nǐ hǎo ma?

B: 我很好。你 呢 ?

Wǒ hěn hǎo. Nǐ ne ?

A: 我也很好。

Wǒ yě hěn hǎo.

Examples

More 呢 (ne) examples (each of these can be translated as a "what about" question):

- 这个很好，那个 呢 ?

  Zhège hěn hǎo, nàge ne ?

  This one is good. What about that one?

- 这个用中文怎么说? 那个 呢 ?

  Zhège yòng Zhōngwén zěnme shuō? Nàge ne ?

  How do I say this in Chinese? And that?

- 我在家，你 呢 ?

  Wǒ zài jiā. Nǐ ne ?

  I'm at home. What about you?

- 你爸爸是上海人，你妈妈 呢 ?

  Nǐ bàba shì Shànghǎi rén, nǐ māma ne ?

  Your father is Shanghainese. And your mom?

- 你哥哥有工作，弟弟 呢 ?

  Nǐ gēge yǒu gōngzuò. Dìdi ne ?

  Your big brother has a job. What about your little brother?

- 北京下雨了。上海 呢 ?

  Běijīng xiàyǔ le. Shànghǎi ne ?

  It's raining in Beijing. How about in Shanghai?

- 我现在要出去。你 呢 ?

  Wǒ xiànzài yào chūqù. Nǐ ne ?

  I'm going to go out now. How about you?

- 我知道你会说中文。你老公 呢 ?

  Wǒ zhīdào nǐ huì shuō Zhōngwén. Nǐ lǎogōng ne ?

  I know you can speak Chinese. What about your husband?

- 这个周末我想去酒吧。你们 呢 ?

  Zhège zhōumò wǒ xiǎng qù jiǔbā. Nǐmen ne ?

  I want to go to a bar this weekend. What about you all?

- 今天晚上没空？明天晚上 呢 ?

  Jīntiān wǎnshang méi kòng? Míngtiān wǎnshang ne ?

  You don't have time tonight? What about tomorrow evening?

Asking "Where" with 呢 (ne)

You'll occasionally hear someone seemingly using 呢 (ne) out of the blue. When this happens, they're usually asking *where* someone or something is, and they expect that you know what they're talking about and know where that person or thing is.

Structure

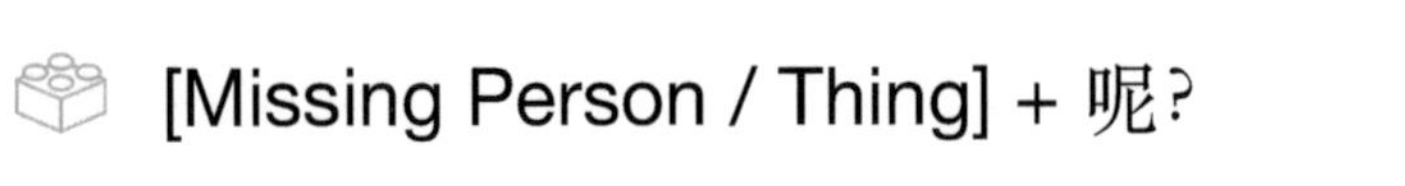

[Missing Person / Thing] + 呢?

Examples

This one is simple, so just a few examples are needed:

- 钱 呢 ?
  Qián ne ?
  Where's the money?
- 你妈妈 呢 ?
  Nǐ māma ne ?
  Where's your mom?
- 我的手机 呢 ?
  Wǒ de shǒujī ne ?
  Where's my cell phone?

Similar to

- Sentence-final interjection "a" (HSK1), page 79
- Yes-no questions with "ma" (HSK1), page 151
- Modal particle "ne" (HSK2)
- Tag questions with "ma" (HSK2)
- Advanced yes-no questions with "ma" (HSK4)
- Softening the tone of questions with "ne" (HSK5)

Sentence-final interjection "a"

The interjection 啊 (a) is often added to the end of sentences to add a tone of urgency, exclamation or excitement. However, the exact meaning often depends on context.

啊 (a) Expressing Exclamation

When used like this, 啊 (a) is placed at the end of a statement and has a tone of exclamation, excitement or enthusiasm. (In a lot of cases, the only English "translation" you can offer is an exclamation point.)

Examples

- 对 啊 ！
  Duì a!
  You're right!

  Banging fist on table...
- 这里好漂亮 啊 ！
  Zhèlǐ hǎo piàoliang a!
  This place is so pretty!
- 你家真大 啊 ！
  Nǐ jiā zhēn dà a!
  Your house is so big.
- 学中文真难 啊 ！
  Xué Zhōngwén zhēn nán a!
  Learning Chinese is so hard!
- 好香 啊 ！什么东西?
  Hǎo xiāng a! Shénme dōngxi?
  It smells great! What is it?

啊 (a) Expressing Certainty or Urgency

啊 (a) can also add a sense of certainty or urgency to a statement, sometimes with the feeling of an order.

Examples

- 是啊，我也觉得！
  Shì a, wǒ yě juéde!
  Definitely, I think so too!
- 行啊！
  Xíng a!
  All right!
- 可以啊！
  Kěyǐ a!
  It's fine!
- 小心啊！
  Xiǎoxīn a!
  Be careful!
- 吃啊！
  Chī a!
  Eat some!

啊 (a) Used in Questions

Finally, it can be used with questions, again with a sense of urgency or concern for the listener.

Examples

- 你走不走啊？
  Nǐ zǒu bu zǒu a?
  Are you going or what?
- 你吃不吃啊？
  Nǐ chī bu chī a?
  Are you eating or not?
- 谁说的啊？
  Shéi shuō de a?
  Who said so?

- 你傻 啊 ？
  Nǐ shǎ a ?
  What are you, stupid?
- 看什么 啊 ？没见过漂亮姑娘 啊 ？
  Kàn shénme a ? Méi jiàn guo piàoliang gūniang a ?
  What are you looking at? Have you never seen a pretty girl before?

Similar to

- Listing things with “a” (HSK5)
- Softening the tone of questions with “ne” (HSK5)
- Expressing the self-evident with “ma” (HSK6)

Softening speech with "ba"

The particle 吧 (ba) can be used to soften the feel of a sentence. This could be to make it more polite, gentler and less forceful, or to turn a command into a suggestion.

Structure

Examples

- 这不太好 吧 。

  Zhè bù tài hǎo ba.

  This isn't so good.
- 算了 吧 。

  Suàn le ba.

  Let's forget it.
- 应该是 吧 。

  Yīnggāi shì ba.

  It should be.
- 钱太少了 吧 。

  Qián tài shǎo le ba.

  It's too little money.
- 再等一等 吧 。

  Zài děng yī děng ba.

  Wait a little longer.
- 太晚了，不要走了 吧 。

  Tài wǎn le, bùyào zǒu le ba.

  It's too late now, don't leave.
- 你们早点来 吧 。

  Nǐmen zǎo diǎn lái ba.

  Come a little earlier.

- 快点 吧 ，要迟到了。
  Kuài diǎn ba, yào chídào le.
  Please hurry, we're going to be late.
- 太贵了 吧 ，我不买了。
  Tài guì le ba, wǒ bù mǎi le.
  It's too expensive. I'm not buying it.
- 那个地方太远了 吧 ，我不想去。
  Nàge dìfang tài yuǎn le ba ， wǒ bù xiǎng qù.
  That place is too far away. I don't want to go.

Similar to

- Suggestions with "ba" (HSK1), page 84
- Conceding with "ba" (HSK2)
- Reduplication of verbs (HSK2, HSK3)
- Softening the tone of questions with "ne" (HSK5)

Suggestions with "ba"

The particle 吧 (ba) has a number of different uses. Here we'll talk about the simplest way to use 吧 (ba): making suggestions.

Structure

Note that in Chinese, whenever you have a command with the subject "we," you're basically just saying, "**let's** (do something)." 吧 (ba) just makes the suggestion sound more tentative and more polite.

Examples

- 我们走 吧 。 *This is a suggestion.*
  Wǒmen zǒu ba .
  Let's go.
- 你说 吧 。 *This is a suggestion.*
  Nǐ shuō ba .
  You say it.
- 快点吃 吧 。 *This is a suggestion.*
  Kuài diǎn chī ba .
  Hurry up and eat.
- 给我两个 吧 。 *This is a suggestion.*
  Gěi wǒ liǎng gè ba .
  Give me two.
- 喝水 吧 。 *This is a suggestion.*
  Hē shuǐ ba .
  Have some water.
- 我们去香港 吧 。 *This is a great suggestion!*
  Wǒmen qù Xiānggǎng ba .
  Let's go to Hong Kong.

- 我们六点去 [吧] ？
  Wǒmen liù diǎn qù [ba]?
  We're going at 6 o'clock (right)?
  This is more of a confirmation than a suggestion.
- 休息一下 [吧] 。
  Xiūxi yīxià [ba].
  Take a break.
  This is a suggestion.
- 我们结婚 [吧] 。
  Wǒmen jiéhūn [ba].
  Let's get married.
  This is a also suggestion, believe it or not!
- 老板，便宜一点 [吧] 。
  Lǎobǎn, piányi yīdiǎn [ba].
  Boss, can you make it cheaper?
  This is more of a request, made to a shopkeeper.

Similar to

- Sentence-final interjection “a” (HSK1), page 79
- Softening speech with “ba” (HSK1), page 82
- Conceding with “ba” (HSK2)
- Reviewing options with “ba” (HSK4)
- Expressing “how about” with “yaobu” (HSK5)

Directional verbs "lai" and "qu"

来 (lái) and 去 (qù) are both words that help to express direction from the perspective of the speaker. 来 (lái) means "come" (towards the speaker), while 去 (qù) means "go" (away from the speaker). For example, if you are in China, a local person might ask you: "When did you come to China?" using 来 (lái). Another example is if you want to go from China to Japan, your friends might ask you: "When are you going to Japan?" using 去 (qù).

Seems really easy, right? Well, learn them well now, because you'll get a lot of mileage out of these words in future grammar patterns.

Basic Usage

Structure

Examples

For the examples below, keep in mind that if the speaker uses 去 (qù), then she is not at the place mentioned *now*. If the speaker uses 来 (lái), she must already be at the place mentioned. Just stay consistent with this, and you're good.

- 妈妈要 去 超市。
  Māma yào qù chāoshì.
  Mom will go to the supermarket.
- 老板今天 来 公司吗?
  Lǎobǎn jīntiān lái gōngsī ma?
  Is the boss coming into the office today?
- 你现在 来 南京路吧。
  Nǐ xiànzài lái Nánjīng Lù ba.
  Come to Nanjing Road now.
- 你不想 来 我们公司工作吗?
  Nǐ bù xiǎng lái wǒmen gōngsī gōngzuò ma?
  Do you not want to come to work for our company?

- 去年她 去 美国工作了几个月。
  Qùnián tā qù Měiguó gōngzuò le jǐ gè yuè.
  Last year she went to work in the USA for a few months.
- 你们想 去 Starbucks 还是 Costa?
  Nǐmen xiǎng qù Starbucks háishì Costa?
  Would you like to go to Starbucks or Costa?
- 周末我喜欢 去 朋友家。
  Zhōumò wǒ xǐhuan qù péngyou jiā.
  I like to go to my friends' places on the weekends.
- 爸爸明天 去 北京出差。
  Bàba míngtiān qù Běijīng chūchāi.
  Dad will go to Beijing on a business trip tomorrow.
- 我今天不上班，你们可以 来 我家吃饭。
  Wǒ jīntiān bù shàngbān, nǐmen kěyǐ lái wǒ jiā chīfàn.
  I don't have to go to work today. You can come to my home to eat dinner.

Advanced Usage

来 (lái) and 去 (qù) can both be paired with other simple verbs to demonstrate the direction an action has taken. For example, 进来 (jìnlái, "come in"), 进去 (jìnqù, "go in"), 出来 (chūlái, "come out"), 出去 (chūqù, "go out"), 回来 (huílái, "come back"), 回去 (huíqù, "go back"), etc.

When you start tacking these two-character verbs onto the ends of other verbs, they are called direction complements, and are covered in detail in a more advanced article.

Expressing existence in a place with "zai"

The verb 在 (zài) expresses existence in a location, similar to how we say in English, "to be at" or "to be in."

Structure

The verb 在 (zài) is used to express existence in a place. English does not have a verb exclusively for this purpose, and instead uses "to be" with a preposition. In Chinese, 在 (zài) can cover both of these roles.

Remember that you don't need another verb in this construction. It can be tempting to try use 是 (shì), as English uses "to be," but this is not correct. 在 (zài) is the only verb needed.

Examples

- 我 在 上海。
  Wǒ zài Shànghǎi.
  I'm in Shanghai.
- 他们 在 英国。
  Tāmen zài Yīngguó.
  They're in England.
- 老板 在 外面。
  Lǎobǎn zài wàimiàn.
  The boss is outside.
- 他不 在 学校。
  Tā bù zài xuéxiào.
  He's not at school.
- 她现在 在 家吗?
  Tā xiànzài zài jiā ma?
  Is she at home now?
- 你 在 公司吗?
  Nǐ zài gōngsī ma?
  Are you at the office?

Literally, "Are you at the company?"

- 老师不 在 办公室吗？
  Lǎoshī bù zài bàngōngshì ma?
  Is the teacher not in the office?
- 谁 在 楼上？
  Shéi zài lóushàng?
  Who is upstairs?
- 我和朋友 在 酒吧。
  Wǒ hé péngyou zài jiǔbā.
  I'm with a friend at a bar.
- 你们明天 在 北京吗？
  Nǐmen míngtiān zài Běijīng ma?
  Are you guys in Beijing tomorrow?

Similar to

- Indicating location with "zai" before verbs (HSK1), page 114
- Special cases of "zai" following verbs (HSK2)
- Expressing location with "zai… shang / xia / li" (HSK4)
- Idiomatic phrases with "zai" (HSK4)
- Expressing "within" a period of time using "zai… nei" (HSK5)

Expressing existence with "you"

The verb 有 (yǒu), which means "to have," can also be used to express existence. This is similar to saying "there is" or "there are" in English.

Structure

Literally, this structure expresses that a place "has" a thing, which is to say, that thing is in the place.

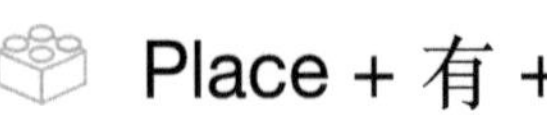

Place + 有 + Obj.

Examples

- 我家 有 很多小狗。
  Wǒ jiā yǒu hěn duō xiǎo gǒu.
  There are a lot of puppies in my home.
- 我们学校 有 很多帅哥。
  Wǒmen xuéxiào yǒu hěn duō shuàigē.
  There are a lot of cute guys in our school.
- 日本 有 很多中国人。
  Rìběn yǒu hěn duō Zhōngguó rén.
  There are many Chinese people in Japan.
- 这个酒吧 有 很多美女。
  Zhège jiǔbā yǒu hěn duō měinǚ.
  There are a lot of pretty girls in this bar.
- 你家 有 牛奶吗?
  Nǐ jiā yǒu niúnǎi ma?
  Is there milk in your house?
- 这里 有 一个问题。
  Zhèlǐ yǒu yī gè wèntí.
  There is a problem here.

- 房间里 有 人吗?
  Fángjiān lǐ yǒu rén ma?
  Is there anyone in the room?
- 杯子里 有 水吗?
  Bēizi lǐ yǒu shuǐ ma?
  Is there any water in the cup?
- 我的手机里 有 你的号码。
  Wǒ de shǒujī lǐ yǒu nǐ de hàomǎ.
  Your number is in my cell phone.
- 现在办公室里 有 人吗?
  Xiànzài bàngōngshì lǐ yǒu rén ma?
  Is there anyone in the office now?

Similar to

- Expressing possession with "you" (HSK1), page 92
- Negation of "you" with "mei" (HSK1), page 15

Expressing possession with "you"

有 (yǒu) can be used in various ways, but the most basic meaning of this verb you need to know is "to have."

Structure

 Subj. + 有 + Obj.

Examples

- 我 有 钱。
  Wǒ yǒu qián.
  I have money.
- 你 有 房子吗?
  Nǐ yǒu fángzi ma?
  Do you have a house?
- 她没 有 车。
  Tā méi yǒu chē.
  She doesn't have a car.
- 他 有 女朋友吗?
  Tā yǒu nǚpéngyou ma?
  Does he have a girlfriend?
- 我们 有 三个女儿。
  Wǒmen yǒu sān gè nǚ'ér.
  We have three daughters.
- 我们家 有 两个公司。
  Wǒmen jiā yǒu liǎng gè gōngsī.
  Our family has two companies.
- 你 有 一百块钱吗?
  Nǐ yǒu yī bǎi kuài qián ma?
  Do you have 100 kuài RMB?

- 你的老师 有 iPad 吗?
  Nǐ de lǎoshī yǒu iPad ma?
  Does your teacher have an iPad?
- 我爸爸没 有 工作。
  Wǒ bàba méi yǒu gōngzuò.
  My dad doesn't have a job.
- 今天你 有 课吗?
  Jīntiān nǐ yǒu kè ma?
  Do you have classes today?

Negating 有 (yǒu)

The verb 有 (yǒu) is negated in a special way. Unlike most verbs, it is negated with 没 (méi) instead of 不 (bù). The negative form of 有 (yǒu) then, is 没有 (méiyǒu). For more on that topic, see our article on negation of "you" with "mei."[1]

Similar to

- Expressing existence with "you" (HSK1), page 90

1. Negation of "you" with "mei" (Grammar), page 15

Polite requests with "qing"

To be more polite in English, we add the word "please" onto our requests. In Chinese, the word 请 (qǐng) serves the same purpose.

Simple Requests

In its most simple form, a polite request can consist of only two words.

Structure

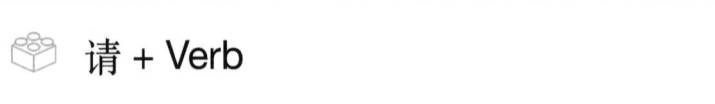

Examples

- 请 进。
  Qǐng jìn.
  Please come in.
- 请 坐。
  Qǐng zuò.
  Please sit down.
- 请 说。
  Qǐng shuō.
  Please speak.

Longer Requests

Obviously, those requests may be significantly longer.

Structure

Examples

- 请 喝茶。
  Qǐng hē chá.
  Please have some tea.

- 请 不要迟到。
  Qǐng bùyào chídào.
  Please do not be late.
- 请 尝一尝。
  Qǐng cháng yī cháng.
  Please have a taste.
- 请 你说得慢一点。
  Qǐng nǐ shuō de màn yīdiǎn.
  Please speak more slowly.
- 请 你听老师的话。
  Qǐng nǐ tīng lǎoshī de huà.
  Please listen to the teacher.
- 请 你离开。
  Qǐng nǐ líkāi.
  Please leave.

The phrase 请问 (qǐngwèn) is a set expression meaning not "please ask," but rather, "may I ask." It frequently comes before asking for directions or other polite requests for information.

- 请 问，洗手间在哪里。
  Qǐng wèn, xǐshǒujiān zài nǎlǐ?
  Excuse me, where is the restroom?

Being Polite without 请 (qǐng)

You may have noticed that the Chinese themselves do not use 请 (qǐng) nearly as much as we use the word "please" in English. It's not because Chinese people are rude; it's because the word 请 (qǐng) feels rather formal in Chinese, and most people don't feel the need to use it with family members, friends, or even co-workers.

Here are some other ways to start make a request to still be polite, but less in a less formal way:

- 你 可不可以 …… ?
  Nǐ kě bu kěyǐ …?
  Could you…?

你 能不能 ……？
Nǐ néng bu néng …?
Can you…?
麻烦 你……
Máfan nǐ…
Can I trouble you to… (?)

More Advanced Uses of 请 (qǐng)

Aside from this "please" usage, the word 请 (qǐng) has some additional uses not covered here. It can mean "to invite," or "to treat (someone to a meal)," and can even be used as a causative verb. None of those uses are covered here.

Using the verb "jiao"

The verb 叫 (jiào) is used to indicate what someone or something is called, or what someone or something's name is. Its usage can seem a little weird to beginners, so it gets its own grammar point.

Structure

The verb 叫 (jiào) means both "to call" and "to be called." It's an easy way to give names, using the following structure:

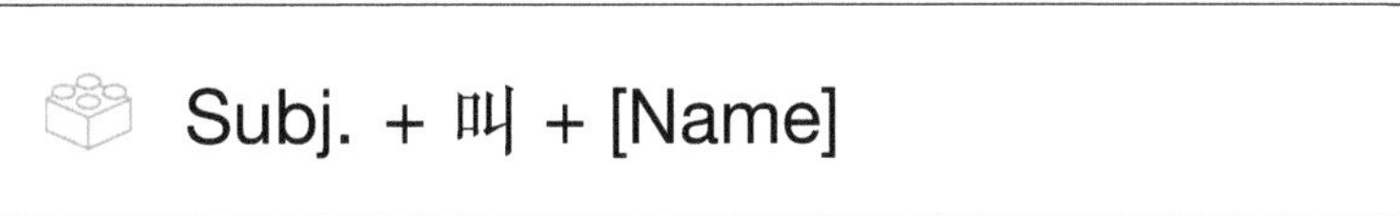

This can be used to give your full name or just your first name.

Examples

- 我 叫 Tom。
  Wǒ jiào Tom.
  My name is Tom.
  Note: it even works if you don't have a Chinese name!
- 他 叫 李小龙。
  Tā jiào Lǐ Xiǎolóng.
  His name is Li Xiaolong.
  Note: this is the real name of Bruce Lee
- 我哥哥 叫 老马。
  Wǒ gēge jiào Lǎo Mǎ.
  My brother is called Lao Ma.
  Note: this is probably not his real name
- 那个 叫 什么?
  Nàge jiào shénme?
  What is that called?
- 这个美女 叫 Alana。
  Zhège měinǚ jiào Alana.
  This pretty girl is named Alana.
- 我们的老板 叫 John。
  Wǒmen de lǎobǎn jiào John.
  Our boss is named John.

- 我的狗 叫 Max。
  Wǒ de gǒu jiào Max.
  My dog is called Max.
- 这种手机 叫 iPhone。
  Zhè zhǒng shǒujī jiào iPhone.
  This kind of cell phone is called an iPhone.
- 你爸爸 叫 什么？
  Nǐ bàba jiào shénme?
  What is your dad's name?
- 这个地方 叫 外滩。
  Zhège dìfang jiào Wàitān.
  This place is called the Bund.

You can also ask people their names using 叫 (jiào):

- 你 叫 什么名字？
  Nǐ jiào shénme míngzi?
  What's your name?

Similar to

- Using the verb "xing" (HSK2)
- Causative verbs (HSK3, HSK4)

Using the verb "qu"

You can use 去 (qù) whenever you have somewhere to go. It's pretty easy to get a handle on this verb; the only trick is getting used to not needing a word for "to" before the destination.

去 (qù) with Just a Place

The verb 去 (qù) means "to go," and is an easy way to talk about going to places.

Structure

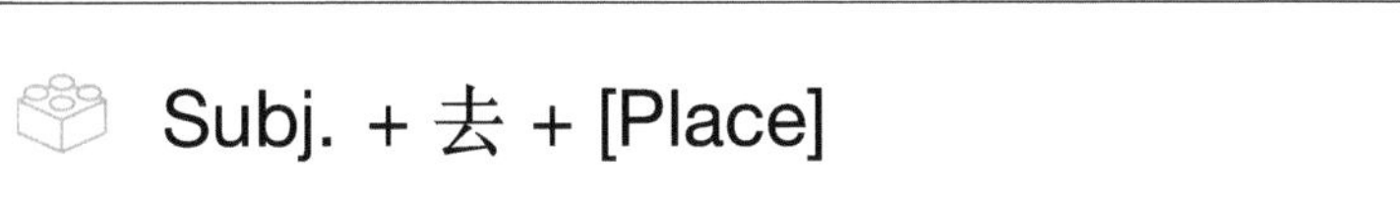

Notice that you don't need a word to express "to."

Examples

公司 literally means "company" but is often used to mean "office."

- 我 去 公司。
  Wǒ qù gōngsī.
  I'm going to the office.
- 你 去 洗手间吗?
  Nǐ qù xǐshǒujiān ma?
  Are you going to the restroom?
- 下午我会 去 超市。
  Xiàwǔ wǒ huì qù chāoshì.
  In the afternoon, I'll go to the supermarket.
- 我们现在 去 公园。
  Wǒmen xiànzài qù gōngyuán.
  We're going to the park now.
- 晚上我们 去 酒吧。你去吗?
  Wǎnshang wǒmen qù jiǔbā. Nǐ qù ma?
  Tonight we're going to the bar. Are you going?

You can also use 去 (qù) for asking questions. (Note the use of question words and question particles.)

A: 你去哪儿？
Nǐ qù nǎr ?
Where are you going?

B: 我去学校。
Wǒ qù xuéxiào .
I am going to school.

A: 你去我家吗？
Nǐ qù wǒ jiā ma ?
Are you going to my place?

B: 我去。
Wǒ qù.
Yes.

literally, "I'm going."

When answering a yes-no question that uses 去 (qù) you don't need anything following it. However, it's important to note that you cannot just use 去 (qù) when there is no context.

去 (qù) with a Verb

Instead of a place, 去 (qù) can also be followed by some sort of action. The structure then means "go to do (something)," and "go and do (something)."

Structure

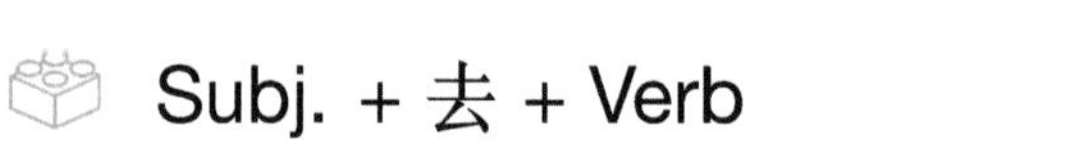

Examples

- 我去工作。
  Wǒ qù gōngzuò.
  I'm going to work.
- 他去上课。
  Tā qù shàngkè.
  He's going to class.

- 你想 去 旅行吗?

  Nǐ xiǎng qù lǚxíng ma?

  Would you like to go travel?

- 我们 去 吃饭吧。

  Wǒmen qù chīfàn ba.

  Let's go eat.

- 九点我们 去 买。

  Jiǔ diǎn wǒmen qù mǎi.

  At 9 o'clock, we'll go buy it.

Similar to

- Using "dao" to mean "to go to" (HSK2)

Expressing "will" with "hui"

会 (huì) has multiple uses, but in this context, it is being used to express the possibility of an action happening in the future.

Basic Usage

Structure

As well as expressing a learned skill[1], 会 (huì) can also be used to indicate that something *will* happen or that someone *will* do something.

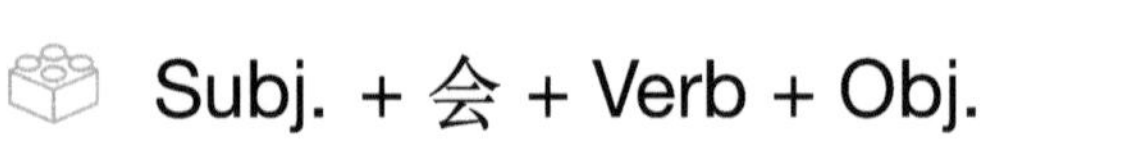

Subj. + 会 + Verb + Obj.

Examples

- 明天你 会 来吗?
  Míngtiān nǐ huì lái ma?
  Will you come tomorrow?
- 他 会 来看你吗?
  Tā huì lái kàn nǐ ma?
  Will he come to see you?
- 明天 会 下雨吗?
  Míngtiān huì xiàyǔ ma?
  Will it rain tomorrow?
- 我出去一下，很快 会 回来。
  Wǒ chūqù yīxià, hěnkuài huì huílái.
  I'm going out for a little while. I'll come back very soon.
- 老板 会 同意吗?
  Lǎobǎn huì tóngyì ma?
  Will the boss agree?
- 你女儿 会 听你的话。
  Nǐ nǚér huì tīng nǐ de huà.
  Your daughter will listen to you.

---

1. Expressing a learned skill with "hui" (Grammar), page 106

- 下班以后，我 会 给你打电话。
  Xiàbān yǐhòu, wǒ huì gěi nǐ dǎ diànhuà.
  After getting off work, I will give you a call.

Negating 会 (huì) with 不 (bù)

Nothing new here. You remember everyone's favorite Negative Nelly 不 (bù)[1], right?

Structure

Subj. + 不 + 会 + Verb + Obj.

Examples

- 我们 不会 告诉你。
  Wǒmen bù huì gàosu nǐ.
  We won't tell you.
- 他 不会 跟你结婚。
  Tā bù huì gēn nǐ jiéhūn.
  He won't marry you.
- 今晚我 不会 在外面吃饭。
  Jīnwǎn wǒ bù huì zài wàimiàn chīfàn.
  Tonight I will not eat out.

Similar to

- Expressing a learned skill with “hui” (HSK1), page 106
- Auxiliary verb “yao” and its multiple meanings (HSK2)
- Wanting to do something with “yao” (HSK2)
- In the future in general with “yihou” (HSK3)
- Expressing future with “jiang” (HSK5)
- The use of Taiwanese Mandarin “hui” (HSK5)
- Expressing “inevitably” with “shibi” (HSK6)

---

1. Standard negation with “bu” (Grammar), page 18

Expressing "would like to" with "xiang"

If you want to express something that you "would like to do," 想 (xiǎng) will be a very helpful auxiliary verb to know. Although similar to 要 (yào), 想 (xiǎng) will give you another more tactful option when you want to articulate a desire.

Basic Usage

Structure

The verb 想 (xiǎng) can be used to express "would like to." In this case it's an auxiliary verb. The structure is:

Examples

- 你想去吗?
  Nǐ xiǎng qù ma?
  Would you like to go?
- 我想吃面。
  Wǒ xiǎng chī miàn.
  I would like to eat noodles.
- 你想喝水吗?
  Nǐ xiǎng hē shuǐ ma?
  Would you like to drink some water?
- 我们想看电视。
  Wǒmen xiǎng kàn diànshì.
  We would like to watch TV.
- 他想买一个大房子。
  Tā xiǎng mǎi yī gè dà fángzi.
  He would like to buy a big apartment.

Negate 想 (xiǎng) with 不 (bù)

No surprises here: use 不 (bù) to negate[1] 想 (xiǎng).

Structure

Subj. + 不 + 想 + Verb + Obj.

Examples

- 他们 不想 去酒吧。
  Tāmen bù xiǎng qù jiǔbā.
  They wouldn't like to go to the bar.
- 你 不想 认识这个美女吗?
  Nǐ bù xiǎng rènshi zhège měinǚ ma?
  Would you not like to know this beautiful lady?
- 我 不想 回家。
  Wǒ bù xiǎng huíjiā.
  I wouldn't like to return home.
- 那个地方很近，我 不想 开车。
  Nàge dìfang hěn jìn, wǒ bù xiǎng kāichē.
  That place is so close. I would not like to drive.
- 他 不想 花父母的钱。
  Tā bù xiǎng huā fùmǔ de qián.
  He would not like to spend his parents' money.

Similar to

- Expressing "be going to" with "yao" (HSK2)

1. Standard negation with "bu" (Grammar), page 18

Expressing a learned skill with "hui"

The word 会 (huì) can be used to express an ability that has been learned (a skill). In this case 会 (huì) is an auxiliary verb.

Basic Usage

Structure

Subj. + 会 + Verb + Obj.

This structure is the easiest way to express all kinds of skills, from languages, to sports, to skills in daily life such as cooking and driving.

Examples

- 他 会 说中文。
  Tā huì shuō Zhōngwén.
  He can speak Chinese.
- 我 会 写汉字。
  Wǒ huì xiě Hànzì.
  I can write Chinese characters.
- 你 会 做饭吗?
  Nǐ huì zuòfàn ma?
  Can you cook food?
- 狗 会 唱歌吗?
  Gǒu huì chànggē ma?
  Can dogs sing?
- 爸爸 会 开车。
  Bàba huì kāichē.
  Dad can drive.

Negating 会 (huì) Sentences

Structure

会 (huì) sentences are negated with 不 (bù)[1], which is inserted in front of 会 (huì):

> Subj. + 不 + 会 + Verb + Obj.

Again, this is the simplest way to express the lack of a learned ability. So while "can't" is a natural translation for "不会" (bù huì) in English, "don't know how to" is equally correct (and perhaps more helpful).

Also, due to a tone change rule for "不" (bù), the phrase "不会" (bù huì) is actually pronounced "bú huì."

Examples

- 我 不会 说英文。
  Wǒ bù huì shuō Yīngwén.
  I can't speak English.
- 妈妈 不会 做中国菜。
  Māma bù huì zuò Zhōngguó cài.
  Mom can't cook Chinese food.
- 你 不会 游泳吗?
  Nǐ bù huì yóuyǒng ma?
  You can't swim?
- 我奶奶 不会 用电脑。
  Wǒ nǎinai bù huì yòng diànnǎo.
  My grandmother can't use a computer.
- 你 不会 开车吗?
  Nǐ bù huì kāichē ma?
  You can't drive a car?

Note that if we say 我不能说中文 (wǒ bù néng shuō Zhōngwén), the speaker is saying that he can't speak Chinese for some reason other than his own ability[2],

1. Standard negation with "bu" (Grammar), page 18
2. Expressing ability or possibility with "neng" (Grammar), page 109

perhaps because speaking Chinese in English class is forbidden.

Similar to

- Expressing “will” with “hui” (HSK1), page 102
- Expressing ability or possibility with “neng” (HSK1), page 109
- Expressing permission with “keyi” (HSK2)

Expressing ability or possibility with "neng"

能 (néng) is one of several Chinese words that is normally translated as "can" in English. However, 能 (néng) is used to emphasize one's ability or the possibility of something happening.

Expressing Ability

能 (néng) indicates ability when used with activities that are not consciously learned or studied.

Structure

The structure to use 能 (néng) to express "ability" is:

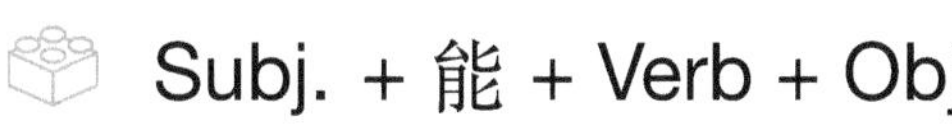

Subj. + 能 + Verb + Obj.

Examples

- 我 能 吃四十个饺子。
  Wǒ néng chī sìshí gè jiǎozi.
  I can eat 40 dumplings.
- 他 能 工作 24 个小时。
  Tā néng gōngzuò èrshí-sì gè xiǎoshí.
  He can work 24 hours.
- 你 能 帮我找到他吗?
  Nǐ néng bāng wǒ zhǎodào tā ma?
  Can you help me find him?
- 你的手机 能 上网吗?
  Nǐ de shǒujī néng shàngwǎng ma?
  Can your cell phone go on the internet?
- 一岁的宝宝 能 说话吗?
  Yī suì de bǎobao néng shuōhuà ma?
  Can a one year old baby talk?

Expressing Possibility

When used with activities that are consciously learned or studied, 能 (néng) generally means that circumstances do not allow execution of the action. In other words, it's *not possible.*

Structure

The structure to use 能 (néng) to express possibility is exactly the same:

> Subj. + 能 + Verb + Obj.

Examples

- 开车一个小时 能 到家吗?
  Kāichē yī gè xiǎoshí néng dào jiā ma?
  Is it possible to drive home in one hour?
- 他们明天 能 早点来吗?
  Tāmen míngtiān néng zǎo diǎn lái ma?
  Would it be possible for them to come a little earlier tomorrow?
- 你们 能 小声一点吗?
  Nǐmen néng xiǎo shēng yīdiǎn ma?
  Could you all lower your voices a bit?
- 你 能 告诉我她的手机号码吗?
  Nǐ néng gàosu wǒ tā de shǒujī hàomǎ ma?
  Could you tell me her cell phone number?
- 一千块 能 买一个手机吗?
  Yīqiān kuài néng mǎi yī gè shǒujī ma?
  Is it possible to buy a cell phone with one thousand RMB?

Other Usages

From these examples we can see such circumstances might be pertaining to getting someone's consent or reliant on the speaker's health. If the speaker wishes to express that they are able to execute an action requiring a consciously studied skill, 会 (huì) can be used instead.

Because 能 (néng) can express possibility, it is often used to form polite questions, something like "would it be possible" in English:

Examples

- 我 能 问你一个问题吗?
  Wǒ néng wèn nǐ yī gè wèntí ma?
  Could I ask you a question?
- 我 能 坐在这里吗?
  Wǒ néng zuò zài zhèlǐ ma?
  Could I sit here?
- 这里不 能 游泳。
  Zhèlǐ bù néng yóuyǒng.
  You can't swim here.
  It's not allowed, or not possible for other reasons.
- 上课的时候不 能 说英文。
  Shàngkè de shíhou bù néng shuō Yīngwén.
  In class, you can't speak English.
  My teacher has forbidden me from speaking English.
- 工作的时候不 能 玩手机。
  Gōngzuò de shíhou bù néng wán shǒujī.
  When working, you can't play with your cell phone.

Similar to

- Expressing a learned skill with "hui" (HSK1), page 106
- Expressing permission with "keyi" (HSK2)

How to do something with "zenme"

怎么 (zěnme) means "how" in Chinese, and it's not hard to use at all: just put it before a verb.

The Basic "How to Verb" Usage

Structure

The question word 怎么 (zěnme) is used to ask *how* in Chinese. It is inserted in front of the verb that's being asked about:

Note that the subject can often be omitted from general "how to" questions, and there doesn't always have to be an object.

Examples

- 你们 怎么 学中文?
  Nǐmen zěnme xué Zhōngwén?
  How do you study Chinese?
- 你 怎么 上班? 坐地铁吗?
  Nǐ zěnme shàngbān? Zuò dìtiě ma?
  How do you get to work? By metro?
- 你知道 怎么 去外滩吗?
  Nǐ zhīdào zěnme qù Wàitān ma?
  Do you know how to get to the Bund?
- 你 怎么 知道我喜欢旅行?
  Nǐ zěnme zhīdào wǒ xǐhuan lǚxíng?
  How did you know I like to travel?
- 我不知道 怎么 跟女孩子说话。
  Wǒ bù zhīdào zěnme gēn nǚháizi shuōhuà.
  I don't know how to talk to girls.

Topic First

Starting a "how to" question with the topic at the beginning of the question is very common. That is, the thing being asked about is introduced first, then a question is asked about how to do something involving it.

Structure

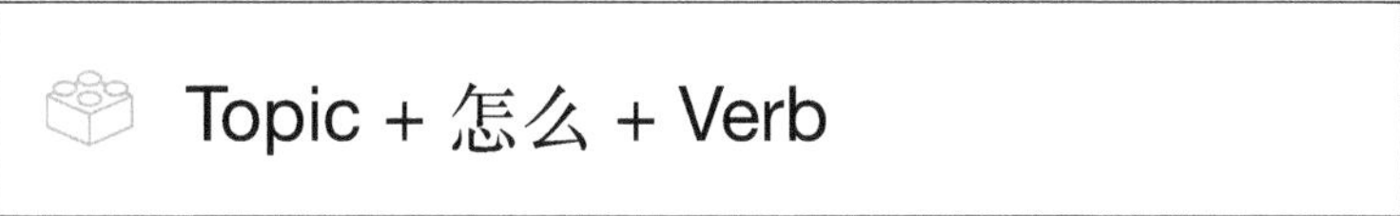

The object doesn't have to come after the verb. Sometimes it moves to the front of the question, establishing what the question is going to be about, before getting specific with the "how" question.

Examples

- 芒果 怎么 吃?
  Mángguǒ zěnme chī?
  How do you eat mangos?
- iPad 怎么 用?
  iPad zěnme yòng?
  How do you use an iPad?
- 语法 怎么 学?
  Yǔfǎ zěnme xué?
  How do you study grammar?
- 中国菜 怎么 做?
  Zhōngguó cài zěnme zuò?
  How do you cook Chinese food?
- "Apple" 怎么 说?
  "Apple" zěnme shuō?
  How do you say apple?

  the "in Chinese" is implied

Similar to

- Asking how something is with "zenmeyang" (HSK1), page 136
- Placement of question words (HSK1), page 138
- Asking why with "zenme" (HSK2)

Indicating location with "zai" before verbs

If you need to include the place where an action takes place, you can use 在 (zài). Just pay close attention to word order[1], as this is one case in which Chinese word order is quite different from English.

Structure

To indicate the location that a verb takes place in, 在 (zài), followed by a location, comes before the verb.

Subj. + 在 + Place + Verb + Obj.

Notice that the location is placed *before* the verb in Chinese, whereas in English it appears *afterwards*.

Examples

- 我在上海上大学。
  Wǒ zài Shànghǎi shàng dàxué.
  I went to college in Shanghai.
- 你一直在这家公司工作吗?
  Nǐ yīzhí zài zhè jiā gōngsī gōngzuò ma?
  Have you always been working in this company?
- 我周末想在家睡觉。
  Wǒ zhōumò xiǎng zài jiā shuìjiào.
  On the weekend, I want to sleep at home.
- 不要在床上吃东西。
  Bù yào zài chuáng shàng chī dōngxi.
  Don't eat food on the bed.
  In addition to "在" you need a "上" to indicate the location "on the bed."
- 你想在哪儿开生日派对?
  Nǐ xiǎng zài nǎr kāi shēngrì pàiduì?
  Where do you want to have the birthday party?

1. Basic sentence order (Grammar), page 118

- 他喜欢 在 厕所里 抽烟。

  Tā xǐhuan zài cèsuǒ lǐ chōuyān.

  He likes to smoke in the bathroom.

  In addition to "在" you need a "里" to indicate the location "in the bathroom."

- 很多人 在 地铁上 吃早饭。

  Hěn duō rén zài dìtiě shàng chī zǎofàn.

  Many people eat breakfast on the subway.

  In addition to "在" you need a "上" to indicate the location "in the subway."

- 现在我们 在 KTV 唱歌。

  Xiànzài wǒmen zài KTV chànggē.

  Now we're singing songs at karaoke.

- 老板 在 会议室 见客户。

  Lǎobǎn zài huìyìshì jiàn kèhù.

  The boss is seeing the client in the meeting room.

- 你 在 外面 吃过晚饭了吗?

  Nǐ zài wàimiàn chī guo wǎnfàn le ma?

  Did you eat dinner outside?

Remember: in English we usually put the location at the end of a sentence. In Chinese, we put the location after the subject but *before* the verb.

Getting More Specific with Locations

Rather than just using 在 (zài) to mean "at" a location, you might want to use it to mean "in," "on," or "under" a specific location. To do this, you'll need to add an extra word after the location. Learn about expressing location with "zai… shang / xia / li".

Similar to

- Basic sentence order (HSK1), page 118
- Expressing existence in a place with "zai" (HSK1), page 88
- Time words and word order (HSK1), page 38
- Special cases of "zai" following verbs (HSK2)
- Using "dao" to mean "to go to" (HSK2)
- Expressing location with "zai… shang / xia / li" (HSK4)
- Expressing "within" a period of time using "zai… nei" (HSK5)

Negation of past actions with "meiyou"

Use 没有 (méiyǒu) to negate past actions (to say that someone *didn't do* something, or something *didn't happen*).

Structure

Usually verbs can be negated with 不 (bù)[1], but that construction is used for habitual or present actions. If the verb is about an action **in the past**, though, 没有 (méiyǒu) should be used:

Note that you can shorten 没有 (méiyǒu) to just 没 (méi).

Examples

- 我 没有 去上班。
  Wǒ méiyǒu qù shàngbān.
  I didn't go to work.
- 他们 没有 说话。
  Tāmen méiyǒu shuōhuà.
  They didn't speak.
- 我 没有 喝你的啤酒。
  Wǒ méiyǒu hē nǐ de píjiǔ.
  I didn't drink your beer.
- 她 没有 看到你。
  Tā méiyǒu kàndào nǐ.
  She didn't see you.
- 我 没有 吃早饭。
  Wǒ méiyǒu chī zǎofàn.
  I didn't eat breakfast.

---

1. Standard negation with "bu" (Grammar), page 18

- 宝宝 没 哭。
  Bǎobao méi kū.
  The baby didn't cry.

有 has been omitted here.

- 你昨天 没 回家吗?
  Nǐ zuótiān méi huíjiā ma?
  You didn't go back home yesterday?
- 老板今天 没 来吗?
  Lǎobǎn jīntiān méi lái ma?
  The boss didn't come today?
- 老师今天 没 生气。
  Lǎoshī jīntiān méi shēngqì.
  The teacher didn't get angry today.
- 妈妈晚上 没 做饭。
  Māma wǎnshang méi zuòfàn.
  Mom didn't cook food this evening.

Go Easy on the 了 (le)

One thing you need to remember when using 没有 (méiyǒu) is that **了 (le) is not normally used with 没有 (méiyǒu)**. 了 (le) marks completed actions, while 没有 (méiyǒu) is used for actions that *didn't happen* (so of course they're not completed). These two don't work together. This is a very common mistake for beginner learners of Chinese.

✘ 我 没有 做 了 。

Wǒ méiyǒu zuò le .

✔ 我 没有 做。
Wǒ méiyǒu zuò.
I didn't do it.

Similar to

- Comparing "bu" and "mei" (HSK1), page 161
- Negation of "you" with "mei" (HSK1), page 15
- Standard negation with "bu" (HSK1), page 18

Basic sentence order

In its most basic form, Chinese word order is very similar to English word order. These similarities definitely have their limits, though; don't expect the two languages' word orders to stay consistent much beyond the very basic sentence orders outlined below.

Subject-Predicate

A simple predicate can be just a verb. The most basic word order in Chinese is:

Structure

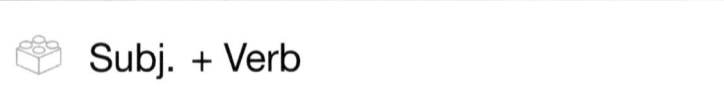

You can form very simple sentences with just two words.

Examples

Subject	Verb	Translation
你们 Nǐmen	吃。 chī.	You eat.
他 Tā	笑。 xiào.	He laughs.
我 Wǒ	读。 dú.	I read.
你 Nǐ	去。 qù.	You go.
你们 Nǐmen	看。 kàn.	You look.
你 Nǐ	来。 lái.	You come here!
我 Wǒ	说。 shuō.	I speak.
孩子 Háizi	哭。 kū.	Children cry.

谁 Shéi	要学? yào xué?	Who wants to study?
谁 Shéi	想玩? xiǎng wán?	Who wants to play?

Subject-Verb-Object

A slightly longer predicate might be a verb with an object. A sentence with both a verb and an object is formed with this structure:

Structure

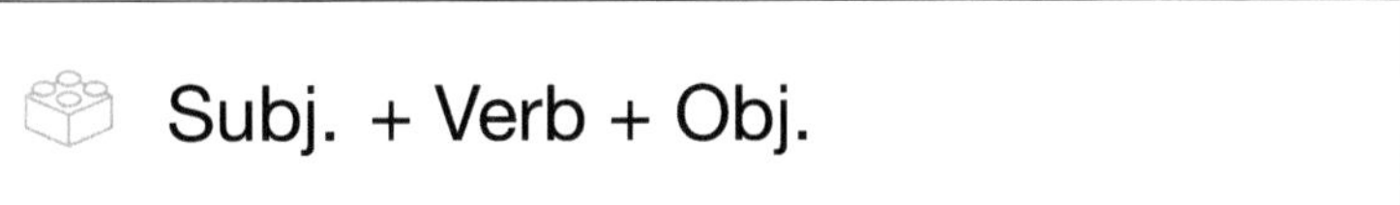

This is the same as in English, and is commonly referred to as SVO word order. You can express a huge variety of things with this simple structure.

Examples

Subject	Verb	Object	Translation
他们 Tāmen	吃 chī	肉。 ròu.	They eat meat.
你 Nǐ	喝 hē	茶吗? chá ma?	Do you drink tea?
我 Wǒ	去 qù	学校。 xuéxiào.	I go to school.
他 Tā	说 shuō	中文。 Zhōngwén.	He speaks Chinese.
你 Nǐ	喜欢 xǐhuan	孩子吗? háizi ma?	Do you like kids?
我们 Wǒmen	要买 yào mǎi	电脑。 diànnǎo.	We want to buy a computer.
你们 Nǐmen	想吃 xiǎng chī	中国菜吗? Zhōngguó cài ma?	Do you want to eat Chinese food?

我 Wǒ	爱 ài	你和爸爸。 nǐ hé bàba.	I love you and dad.
他们 Tāmen	要做 yào zuò	什么? shénme?	What do they want to do?
你 Nǐ	想去 xiǎng qù	什么地方? shénme dìfang?	What place do you want to go to?

When Things Get Tricky

Despite the convenient word order similarities highlighted above, things start to break down as soon as you start adding in such simple sentence elements as the "also" adverb 也 (yě)[1], a time word[2], or a location where something happened[3].

Don't worry; the more complicated Chinese structures aren't hard, they're just different! (If Chinese word order were really the same as English word order, that would be just a little too convenient, wouldn't it?)

Similar to

- Connecting nouns with "shi" (HSK1), page 121
- Indicating location with "zai" before verbs (HSK1), page 114
- Placement of question words (HSK1), page 138
- Simple "noun + adjective" sentences (HSK1), page 126
- Standard negation with "bu" (HSK1), page 18
- Actions in a row (HSK2)
- Wanting to do something with "yao" (HSK2)

1. The "also" adverb "ye" (Grammar), page 23
2. Time words and word order (Grammar), page 38
3. Indicating location with "zai" before verbs (Grammar), page 114

Connecting nouns with "shi"

The verb *to be* is not used in Chinese the same way as it is in English. In Chinese, 是 (shì) is for connecting nouns, and is generally not used with adjectives.

Basic Usage

Structure

The structure for connecting nouns with 是 (shì) is:

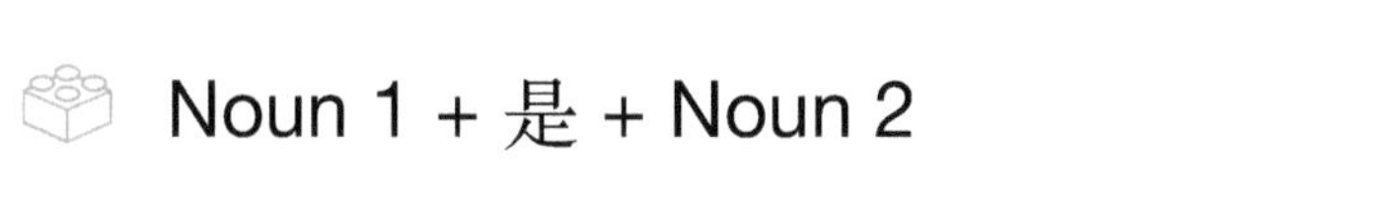

This is equivalent to "Noun 1 **is** Noun 2" in English.

Chinese does not conjugate verbs. That is, the form of the verb is the same no matter who is doing it. In this case, it is always 是 (shì) and never changes. As you can see, it's easy to form simple sentences expressing *to be* in Chinese. The only tricky thing about 是 (shì) in Chinese is that it's used to link *two nouns*, so you can't rely too much on translating directly from English when it comes to expressing the English verb "to be" in Chinese.

Examples

- 我 是 学生。

  Wǒ shì xuésheng.

  I am a student.
- 你 是 John 吗?

  Nǐ shì John ma?

  Are you John?
- 他们 是 有钱人。

  Tāmen shì yǒuqián rén.

  They are rich people.
- 你 是 老板吗?

  Nǐ shì lǎobǎn ma?

  Are you the boss?

- 这 是 我男朋友。
  Zhè shì wǒ nánpéngyou.
  This is my boyfriend.
- 那 是 你们公司吗?
  Nà shì nǐmen gōngsī ma?
  Is that your company?
- 你妈妈 是 老师吗?
  Nǐ māma shì lǎoshī ma?
  Is your mother a teacher?
- 这都 是 你的钱。
  Zhè dōu shì nǐ de qián.
  This is all your money.
- 那 是 什么菜?
  Nà shì shénme cài?
  What food is that?
- 我也 是 他的朋友。
  Wǒ yě shì tā de péngyou.
  I am also his friend.

Other Uses of 是 (shì)

Be careful and take note. As you can see above, 是 (shì) is only used to link two nouns. It can't be used to link a noun and an adjective. This is a very common mistake for people just beginning to learn Chinese. For that kind of sentence, you'll want to use a different structure with the linking word 很 (hěn)[1].

In Chinese it is also possible to use the phrase "是不是 (shì bu shì)?" It can be used at the beginning or end of a sentence. It's meaning is quite similar to the English expressions "right" and "aren't you?" This is very useful if you want to express concern for a person, or if you want to mix up your sentence structure a bit and make it more interesting. The 是不是 (shì bu shì) pattern is also part of affirmative-negative questions.

Another way to use 是 (shì) is to use it as a tag question. You can add "是吗?" (shì ma?) to the end of a question to mean the English equivalent of: "is it" or "yeah?" Using this in a question usually allows the speaker to get a confirmation answer.

---

1. Simple "noun + adjective" sentences (Grammar), page 126

Examples

- 他没听到，是不是？
  Tā méi tīngdào, shì bu shì?
  He didn't hear you, right?
- 你 是不是 还没吃饭？
  Nǐ shì bu shì hái méi chīfàn?
  Haven't you eaten yet?
- 你们 是不是 中国人？
  Nǐmen shì bu shì Zhōngguó rén?
  Are you Chinese?
- 你到了，是吗？
  Nǐ dào le, shì ma?
  You have arrived, yeah?
- 你有两个孩子，是吗？
  Nǐ yǒu liǎng gè háizi, shì ma?
  You have two kids, yeah?

Similar to

- Simple “noun + adjective” sentences (HSK1), page 126
- Standard negation with “bu” (HSK1), page 18

Expressing "excessively" with "tai"

In Chinese, the simplest structure for expressing "too" in the sense of "excessively" is by using the word 太 (tài). Don't forget to also add 了 (le) after the adjective to keep your Chinese sounding natural.

Structure

太 + Adj. + 了

As in English, this can express that something really is excessive (often as a complaint), or can also colloquially express the meaning of "so" or "very."

Examples

The following examples sound a little bit like a complaint, or a reason for not doing something. They're similar to how we would use "too" in English, and the translations are straightforward.

- 米饭太多了。
  Mǐfàn tài duō le.
  There is too much rice.
- 现在太晚了。
  Xiànzài tài wǎn le.
  Now it's too late.
- 老板太忙了。
  Lǎobǎn tài máng le.
  The boss is too busy.
- 老师太累了。
  Lǎoshī tài lèi le.
  The teacher is too tired.
- 这个厕所太脏了。
  Zhège cèsuǒ tài zāng le.
  This restroom is too dirty.

In the following examples, the same exact pattern is used to exclaim how *good* something is, so these uses are totally *not* complaints. The English translations have to get a little more creative to express the same feeling in English.

- 你 太 好 了 。
  Nǐ tài hǎo le.
  You are so great.
- 他 太 帅 了 。
  Tā tài shuài le.
  He is very handsome.
- 这个女孩 太 漂亮 了 。
  Zhège nǚhái tài piàoliang le.
  This girl is so pretty.
- 小猫 太 可爱 了 ！
  Xiǎomāo tài kě'ài le!
  The kitten is so cute!
- 你的孩子 太 聪明 了 。
  Nǐ de háizi tài cōngming le.
  Your kid is wicked smart.

Note for the more advanced learner: This pattern can be used with modal verbs (e.g. 会 (huì), 能 (néng)) as well as psychological verbs (e.g. 喜欢 (xǐhuan), 想 (xiǎng), 爱 (ài)) to intensify the degree.

Source|Modern Mandarin Chinese Grammar: A Practical Guide|57) →buy

Similar to

- Expressing "not very" with "bu tai" (HSK1), page 30
- Expressing "a little too" with "you dian" (HSK2)
- Expressing "really" with "zhen" (HSK2)
- Superlative "zui" (HSK2)
- Adjectives with "-ji le" (HSK3)
- Special verbs with "hen" (HSK3)
- Expressing "quite" with "ting" (HSK4)
- Expressing "a bit too" (HSK5)

Simple "noun + adjective" sentences

In English, nouns can be "linked" to adjectives and other nouns with the verb "to be." In Chinese, nouns are linked to other nouns in one way, but linked to adjectives in a completely different way. Nouns are linked to other nouns with 是 (shì)[1]. Nouns are linked to adjectives with 很 (hěn).

Structure

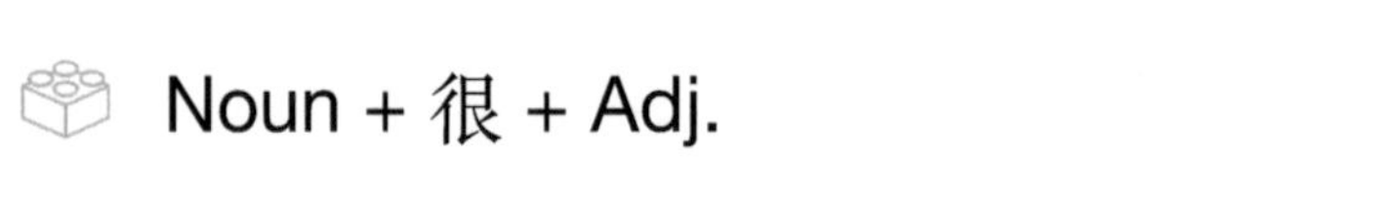
Noun + 很 + Adj.

The noun in this structure is the subject of the sentence. Sometimes the 很 (hěn) in this structure is translated as "very," but often it is just a way to link a noun to an adjective.

Examples

In the following examples, 很 (hěn) is just a link (you could think of it as a substitute for the verb "to be"), and the sentences could be translated as "(Noun) is (adjective)."

- 我很好。
  Wǒ hěn hǎo.
  I'm good.
- 你很漂亮。
  Nǐ hěn piàoliang.
  You are pretty.
- 他很高兴。
  Tā hěn gāoxìng.
  He is happy.
- 中文很难。
  Zhōngwén hěn nán.
  Chinese is difficult.

---

1. Connecting nouns with "shi" (Grammar), page 121

- 老板 很 生气。
  Lǎobǎn hěn shēngqì.
  The boss is angry.
- 我们 很 累。
  Wǒmen hěn lèi.
  We're tired.
- 我哥哥也 很 高。
  Wǒ gēge yě hěn gāo.
  My older brother is also tall.
- 你家也 很 远吗?
  Nǐ jiā yě hěn yuǎn ma?
  Is your house also far away?
- 爸爸 很 忙，妈妈也很忙。
  Bàba hěn máng, māma yě hěn máng.
  Dad is busy, and mom is also busy.
- 他和他弟弟都 很 帅。
  Tā hé tā dìdi dōu hěn shuài.
  He and his younger brother are both handsome.

Remember that **是 (shì) is not used to link adjectives to nouns**. This is a classic mistake that almost everyone makes when learning Chinese. Make sure you use 很 (hěn) and not 是 (shì) to link adjectives to nouns, as shown below:

✘ 他 是 高。
Tā shì gāo.

✔ 他 很 高。
Tā hěn gāo.
He is tall.

What 很 (hěn) Really Means

If you're like most learners, when you first learn this pattern, you're thinking, *"How can 很 (hěn) mean "very" one minute, but then nothing but a "link" the next? How do I know if anything means anything in this language?"* That's a reasonable response. But in the case of these "Noun + Adj." sentences, you just have to think of this usage of 很 (hěn) as an exception. It's just part of the structure.

If you actually want to add the meaning of "very" into the sentence, you could use another adverb instead of 很 (hěn). One good choice is 非常 (fēicháng).

- ✔ 他 非常 高。

  Tā fēicháng gāo.

  He is very tall.

Similar to

- Age with "sui" (HSK1), page 40
- Connecting nouns with "shi" (HSK1), page 121
- The "also" adverb "ye" (HSK1), page 23
- Superlative "zui" (HSK2)
- Adjectives with "name" and "zheme" (HSK3)
- Expressing "both A and B" with "you" (HSK3)
- Reduplication of adjectives (HSK3)
- Special verbs with "hen" (HSK3)
- Emphasizing with "henshi" (HSK6)

Expressing "some" with "yixie"

In order to express "some" or "a few," you can use 一些 (yīxiē). To use it in this way, 一些 (yīxiē) is placed before the noun it modifies. 一些 (yīxiē) can modify the subject or the object.

Note: The pinyin for 一些 is written "yīxiē" but pronounced "yìxiē" due to a tone change rule.

Structure

Examples

- 妈妈去超市买了 一些 水果。
  Māma qù chāoshì mǎi le yīxiē shuǐguǒ.
  Mom went to the supermarket and bought some fruit.
- 上个周末他买了 一些 衣服。
  Shàng gè zhōumò tā mǎi le yīxiē yīfu.
  He bought some clothes last weekend.
- 我们很快会见到 一些 新同事。
  Wǒmen hěn kuài huì jiàndào yīxiē xīn tóngshì.
  We're going to meet some new co-workers very soon.
- 你饿不饿？这里有 一些 吃的。
  Nǐ è bu è? Zhèlǐ yǒu yīxiē chīde.
  Are you hungry or not? There is some food here.
- 下课以后，学生们问了 一些 问题。
  Xiàkè yǐhòu, xuéshengmen wèn le yīxiē wèntí.
  After class, the students asked some questions.
- 给我 一些 时间，好吗？
  Gěi wǒ yīxiē shíjiān, hǎo ma?
  Give me some time, OK?

- 他给我带了 一些 书。
  Tā gěi wǒ dài le yīxiē shū.
  He brought me some books.
- 你可以借我 一些 钱吗?
  Nǐ kěyǐ jiè wǒ yīxiē qián ma?
  Can you lend me some money?
- 你想在咖啡里放 一些 糖吗?
  Nǐ xiǎng zài kāfēi lǐ fàng yīxiē táng ma?
  Do you want to put some sugar in your coffee?
- 我在中国的时候，去过 一些 很漂亮的地方。
  Wǒ zài Zhōngguó de shíhou, qù guo yīxiē hěn piàoliang de dìfang.
  When I was in China, I went to some beautiful places.

Similar to

- Using “ji” to mean “several” (HSK2)
- Using “youde” to mean “some” (HSK3)

Counting money

Cash is king, even though China is now crazy for mobile payments. Either way, though, mastering how to say quantities of money is vital!

Asking "How Much Money" with 多少钱 (duōshao qián)

Before you learn how to count money in Chinese, make sure you know how to ask "how much money" when you go shopping in China.

Structure

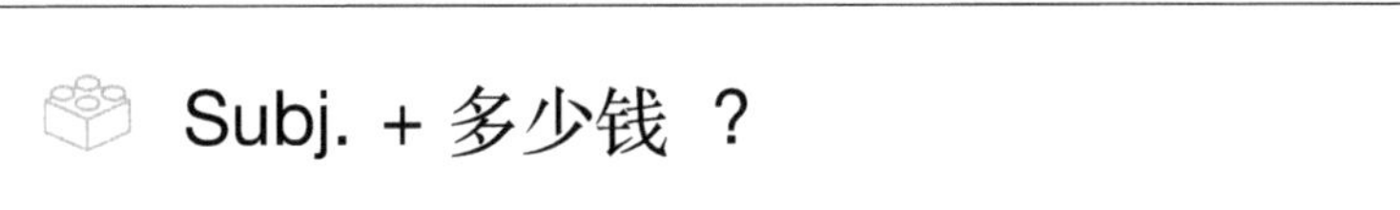

Examples

- 多少钱？
  Duōshao qián?
  How much?
- 你的手机多少钱？
  Nǐ de shǒujī duōshao qián?
  How much was your cell phone?
- 我们的午饭多少钱？
  Wǒmen de wǔfàn duōshao qián?
  How much is our lunch?
- 这杯咖啡多少钱？
  Zhè bēi kāfēi duōshao qián?
  How much for this cup of coffee?
- 这件衣服多少钱？
  Zhè jiàn yīfu duōshao qián?
  How much is this clothing?

Stating Quantities of Money

Structure

Chinese has a specific structure for talking about quantities for money:

 Number + 块 + Number + 毛

Examples

- 两 块 五 毛
  liǎng kuài wǔ máo
  two kuai five mao (2.5)
- 三 块 八 毛
  sān kuài bā máo
  three kuai eight mao (3.8)
- 十 块 两 毛
  shí kuài liǎng máo
  ten kuai two mao (10.2)
- 二十三 块 八 毛
  èrshí-sān kuài bā máo
  Twenty-three kuai eight mao (23.8)
- 五十 块 五 毛
  wǔshí kuài wǔ máo
  fifty kuai five mao (50.5)

Note that "2.5 RMB" reads as 两块五 (liǎng kuài wǔ).

✗ 二 块 五
èr kuài wǔ

✓ 两 块 五
liǎng kuài wǔ
two kuai five mao (2.5)

If the smaller units are only in tens, you can just say the number of tens. So "3.8 RMB" is 三块八 (sān kuài bā). This way of giving the price is normally only used for amounts under 100 RMB.

When the smallest unit is 2, it reads as 二 (èr) instead of 两 (liǎng).

✗ 两 块 两
liǎng kuài liǎng

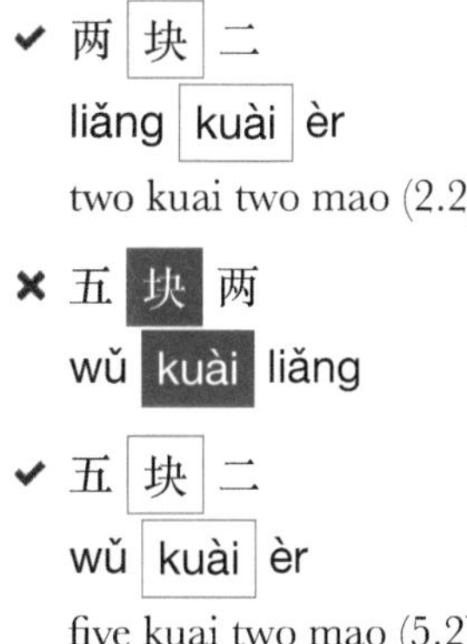

- ✔ 两 块 二
  liǎng kuài èr
  two kuai two mao (2.2)
- ✘ 五 块 两
  wǔ kuài liǎng
- ✔ 五 块 二
  wǔ kuài èr
  five kuai two mao (5.2)

The first number is the amount of whole RMB (or dollars etc.), and the second is the amount smaller units (e.g. cents). So "3.86 RMB" is

- 三 块 八毛六
  sān kuài bā máo liù
  three kuai eight mao six fen (3.86)

And if there's no smaller unit, e.g. "3 RMB," you can just say:

- 三 块
  sān kuài
  Three kuai

块 (kuài) is the more common, informal way to talk about money. More formally you can use 元 (yuán) in exactly the same way. This is similar to the difference between "dollars" and "bucks" in American English, or "pounds" and "quid" in British English. 块 (kuài) is appropriate in more situations than "bucks" or "quid," though.

Similar to

- Indicating a number in excess (HSK2)
- Approximating with sequential numbers (HSK3)

Measure words in quantity questions

Quantity questions are phrases for asking questions like "how much?" or "how many?" You'll need to use the question word[1] 几 (jǐ) with measure words for this.

Asking About Small Numbers with 几 (jǐ)

Structure

You can use the quantity question word[1] 几 (jǐ) instead of a number to ask about quantity with measure words.

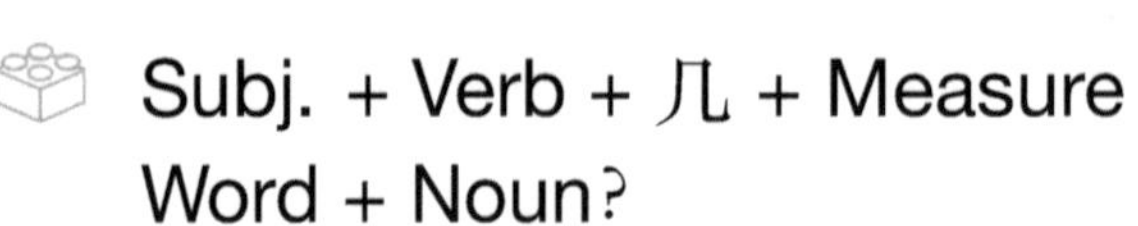

Subj. + Verb + 几 + Measure Word + Noun?

Examples

- 他有 几 个孩子?
  Tā yǒu jǐ gè háizi?
  How many kids does he have?
- 你家有 几 个房间?
  Nǐ jiā yǒu jǐ gè fángjiān?
  How many rooms are there in your house?
- 他们在这里住 几 个星期?
  Tāmen zài zhèlǐ zhù jǐ gè xīngqī?
  How many weeks are they staying here?
- 你带了 几 件衣服?
  Nǐ dài le jǐ jiàn yīfu?
  How many pieces of clothing have you brought?
- 老板每天工作 几 个小时?
  Lǎobǎn měi tiān gōngzuò jǐ gè xiǎoshí?
  How many hours does the boss work every day?

1. Placement of question words (Grammar), page 138

Asking About Big Numbers with 多少 (duōshao)

When the number is not certain but you assume it's definitely more than ten, it's better to ask the question with 多少 (duōshao) instead of 几 (jǐ).

Structure

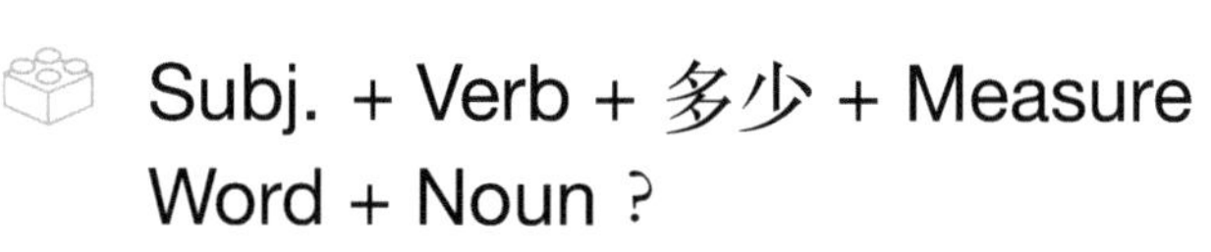
Subj. + Verb + 多少 + Measure Word + Noun ?

Examples

- 你去过 多少 个国家?
  Nǐ qù guo duōshao gè guójiā?
  How many countries have you been to?
- 你们班有 多少 个学生?
  Nǐmen bān yǒu duōshao gè xuéshēng?
  How many students are there in your class?
- 你大学的时候看了 多少 本书?
  Nǐ dàxué de shíhou kàn le duōshao běn shū?
  How many books did you read when you were in college?
- 他们昨天请了 多少 个朋友?
  Tāmen zuótiān qǐng le duōshao gè péngyou?
  How many friends did they invite yesterday?
- 上海有 多少 个外国公司?
  Shànghǎi yǒu duōshao gè wàiguó gōngsī?
  How many foreign companies are there in Shanghai?

Similar to

- Age with "sui" (HSK1), page 40
- Measure word "ge" (HSK1), page 42
- Measure words for counting (HSK2)
- Measure words for verbs (HSK2)
- Measure words with "this" and "that" (HSK2)

Asking how something is with "zenmeyang"

You may know that 怎么 (zěnme) can mean "how"[1], but by adding to it and making it 怎么样 (zěnmeyàng), you can ask *how something is*, or ***what it is like***. This is useful in all manner of conversations, and is essential for building conversation skills.

Basic Usage

Structure

This question form is super simple. It is similar to asking the question, "how is…?"

Examples

Many of these sample sentences are super common in everyday life, so it's a good idea to get familiar with them.

- 你最近 怎么样 ?

  Nǐ zuìjìn zěnmeyàng ?

  How have you been recently?

- 中国 怎么样 ?

  Zhōngguò zěnmeyàng ?

  How is China?

- 北京冬天 怎么样 ?

  Běijīng dōngtiān zěnmeyàng ?

  How is Beijing in the winter?

- 今天天气 怎么样 ?

  Jīntiān tiānqì zěnmeyàng ?

  How is the weather today?

- 你妹妹的工作 怎么样 ?

  Nǐ mèimei dē gōngzuò zěnmeyàng ?

  How is your little sister's job going?

---

1. How to do something with "zenme" (Grammar), page 112

- 你的新手机 怎么样 ?
  Nǐ de xīn shǒujī zěnmeyàng ?
  How's your new phone?
- 这里的菜 怎么样 ? 好吃吗?
  Zhèlǐ de cài zěnmeyàng ? Hǎochī ma?
  How is the food here? is it good?

Asking Opinions

Structure

In this pattern, you're directly asking for an opinion in an open-ended way.

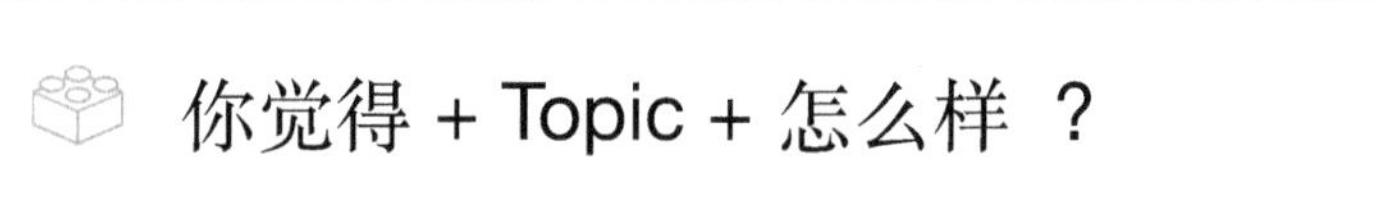

This is like asking, "what do you think of…?"

Examples

- 你觉得 上海 怎么样 ?
  Nǐ juéde Shànghǎi zěnmeyàng ?
  What do you think of Shanghai?
- 你觉得 我 怎么样 ?
  Nǐ juéde wǒ zěnmeyàng ?
  What do you think of me?
- 你觉得 中文 怎么样 ? 难学吗?
  Nǐ juéde Zhōngwén zěnmeyàng? Nánxué ma?
  What do you think of Chinese? is it difficult to learn?

Placement of question words

Who, *what*, *when*, *where*, *why*, and *how*: these question words are all used when forming questions in Chinese. The important thing to remember is that word order is the same in Chinese for questions and statements.

Overview

Common Question Words List

In English, question words are also known as *wh-words*, as the majority of them begin with *wh*:

- 什么

  shénme

  what

- 哪里、哪儿

  nǎlǐ, nǎr

  where

- 哪个

  nǎge

  which

- 谁

  shéi

  who

In spoken Chinese, people normally say "shéi," not "shuí"

- 什么时候

  shénme shíhou

  when

- 为什么

  wèishénme

  why

- 怎么

  zěnme

  how

- 多少

  duōshao

  how many / how much

Rules

In English, question words have to be placed at the beginning of the sentence. This involves changing the word order to allow this rearrangement. In Chinese, using question words is a lot simpler. You simply place a question word in the place of the thing you want to ask about. *Nothing needs to be rearranged.*

So if the statement is

- 我是 小李 。
  Wǒ shì Xiǎo Lǐ.
  I am Xiao Li.

the question form - "who are you?" - has the same word order:

- 你是 谁 ?
  Nǐ shì shéi?
  Who are you? (you are who?)

This works for whatever it is you want to ask about. The question form has the same word order as the statement form.

Expressing "What" with 什么 (shénme)

Structure

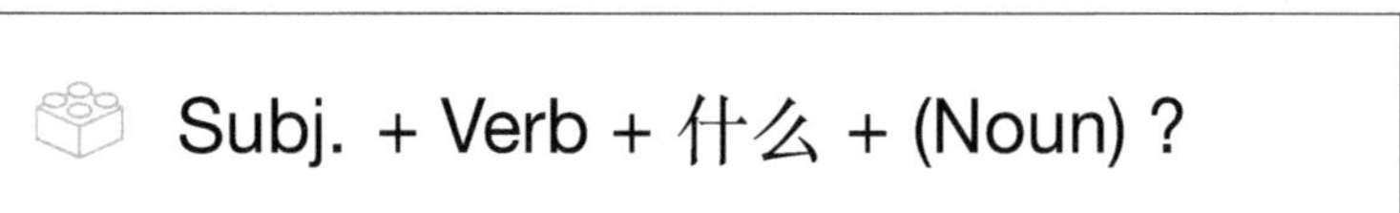

Examples

A: 这是 什么 ?
Zhè shì shénme?
What is this?

B: 这是 我的 iPad 。
Zhè shì wǒ de iPad.
This is my iPad.

A: 你喜欢吃 什么 菜?
Nǐ xǐhuan chī shénme cài?
What kind of food do you like?

B: 我喜欢吃 中国菜 。

Wǒ xǐhuan chī Zhōngguó cài.

I like Chinese food.

A: 你用 什么 手机?

Nǐ yòng shénme shǒujī?

What kind of cell phone do you use?

B: 我用 iPhone 。

Wǒ yòng iPhone.

I use an iPhone.

A: 你在看 什么 书?

Nǐ zài kàn shénme shū?

What kind of book are you reading?

B: 我在看 小说 。

Wǒ zài kàn xiǎoshuō.

I am reading a novel.

A: 他开 什么 车?

Tā kāi shénme chē?

What kind of car does he drive?

B: 他开 宝马 。

Tā kāi Bǎomǎ.

He drives a BMW.

Expressing "Where" with 哪里 (nǎlǐ) / 哪儿 (nǎr)

The words 哪里 (nǎlǐ) and 哪儿 (nǎr) mean the same thing. The difference is simply regional preference: 哪里 (nǎlǐ) is preferred in the south (Shanghai, Taiwan), whereas 哪儿 (nǎr) is preferred in the north (Beijing, Xi'an).

Structure

Subj. + Verb + 哪里 / 哪儿 ?

Examples

A: 你在 哪里 ?
Nǐ zài nǎlǐ?
Where are you?

B: 我在 家 。
Wǒ zài jiā.
I'm at home.

A: 你要去 哪儿 ?
Nǐ yào qù nǎr?
Where are you going now?

B: 我要去 洗手间 。
Wǒ yào qù xǐshǒujiān.
I'm going to the bathroom.

A: 我们在 哪儿 ?
Wǒmen zài nǎr?
Where are we?

B: 我们在 南京西路 。
Wǒmen zài Nánjīng Xī Lù.
We are at West Nanjing road.

A: 这个周末你想去 哪儿 ?
Zhège zhōumò nǐ xiǎng qù nǎr?
Where do you want to go this weekend?

B: 我想去 公园 。
Wǒ xiǎng qù gōngyuán.
I want to go to the park.

A: 你好，你要去 哪儿 ?
Nǐhǎo, nǐ yào qù nǎr?
Hello, where do you want to go?

B: 我要去 外滩 。
Wǒ yào qù Wàitān.
I want to go to the Bund.

Expressing "Which" with 哪个 (nǎge)

Structure

 Subj. + Verb + 哪个 (+ Noun) ?

Examples

A: 你要 哪个 ？
Nǐ yào nǎge?
Which one do you want?

B: 我要 这个 。
Wǒ yào zhège.
I want this one.

A: 你喜欢 哪个菜 ？
Nǐ xǐhuan nǎge cài?
Which dish do you like?

B: 我喜欢 这个菜 。
Wǒ xǐhuan zhège cài.
I like this dish.

A: 我们去 哪个饭店 ？
Wǒmen qù nǎge fàndiàn?
Which restaurant are we going to?

B: 我们去 你妈妈的饭店 。
Wǒmen qù nǐ māma de fàndiàn.
We are going to your mom's restaurant.

A: 你在 哪个房间 ？
Nǐ zài nǎge fángjiān?
Which room are you in?

B: 我在 你的房间 。
Wǒ zài nǐ de fángjiān.
I'm in your room.

A: 你住在 哪个区 ？
Nǐ zhù zài nǎge qū ?
Which district do you live in?

B: 我住在 静安区 。
Wǒ zhù zài Jìng'ān Qū .
I live in Jing'an District.

Expressing "Who" with 谁 (shéi)

Structure

Subj. + 是 + 谁 ？

谁 + Verb ?

Examples

A: 你是 谁 ？
Nǐ shì shéi ?
Who are you?

B: 我是 他女朋友 。
Wǒ shì tā nǚpéngyou .
I'm his girlfriend.

A: 她是 谁 ？
Tā shì shéi ?
Who is she?

B: 她是 我的老师 。
Tā shì wǒ de lǎoshī .
She's my teacher.

A: 你不喜欢 谁 ？
Nǐ bù xǐhuan shéi ?
Who do you not like?

B: 我不喜欢 我的老板 。
Wǒ bù xǐhuan wǒ de lǎobǎn.
I don't like my boss.

A: 谁 想去？
Shéi xiǎng qù?
Who wants to go?

B: 我 想去。
Wǒ xiǎng qù.
I want to go.

A: 谁 想喝咖啡？
Shéi xiǎng hē kāfēi?
Who wants to drink coffee?

B: 我 想喝咖啡。
Wǒ xiǎng hē kāfēi.
I want to drink coffee.

Expressing "When" with 什么时候 (shénme shíhou)

Structure

 Subj. + 什么时候 + Predicate ?

Examples for asking and telling *when* (to keep things simple, we'll just include questions about the future; asking questions about the past can be slightly more complicated and may involve the "shi… de" construction).

Examples

A: 你 什么时候 来？
Nǐ shénme shíhou lái?
When are you coming?

B: 我 明天 来。
Wǒ míngtiān lái.
I'm coming tomorrow.

A: 你们 什么时候 走?
Nǐmen shénme shíhou zǒu?
When are you guys leaving?

B: 我们 下个月 走。
Wǒmen xià gè yuè zǒu.
We're leaving next month.

A: 我们 什么时候 吃饭?
Wǒmen shénme shíhou chīfàn?
When are we eating?

B: 我们 6 点 吃饭。
Wǒmen liù diǎn chīfàn.
We're eating at 6:00.

A: 爸爸 什么时候 回来?
Bàba shénme shíhou huílái?
When is dad coming back?

B: 爸爸 周末 回来。
Bàba zhōumò huílái.
Dad is coming back this weekend.

A: 你的飞机 什么时候 到上海?
Nǐ de fēijī shénme shíhou dào Shànghǎi?
When is your airplane arriving in Shanghai?

B: 晚上八点 。
Wǎnshang bā diǎn.
Eight o'clock this evening.

Expressing "Why" with 为什么 (wèishénme)

Structure

 Subj. + 为什么 + Predicate ?

Examples

A: 你 为什么 学中文?
Nǐ wèishénme xué Zhōngwén?
Why do you study Chinese?

B: 因为 我在中国工作。
Yīnwèi wǒ zài Zhōngguó gōngzuò.
Because I'm working in China.

A: 他们 为什么 不喝咖啡?
Tāmen wèishénme bù hē kāfēi?
Why don't you drink coffee?

B: 因为 咖啡很苦。
Yīnwèi kāfēi hěn kǔ.
Because coffee is bitter.

A: 他 为什么 不来?
Tā wèishénme bù lái?
Why isn't he coming?

B: 因为 他很忙。
Yīnwèi tā hěn máng.
Because he is busy.

A: 你早上 为什么 不在?
Nǐ zǎoshang wèishénme bù zài?
Why were you not here this morning?

B: 因为 我出去见朋友了。
Yīnwèi wǒ chūqù jiàn péngyou le.
Because I went out to meet some friends.

A: 这些外国人 为什么 不喜欢中国?
Zhèxiē wàiguó rén wèishénme bù xǐhuan Zhōngguó?
Why do these foreigners not like China?

B: 因为 中国人太多。
Yīnwèi Zhōngguó rén tài duō.
Because China has a lot of people.

Expressing "How" with 怎么 (zěnme)

Structure

 Subj. + 怎么 + Verb (+ Obj.) ?

Examples

A: 你 怎么 学习中文?
Nǐ zěnme xuéxí Zhōngwén?
How do you study Chinese?

B: 我 用 Grammar Wiki 学习中文。
Wǒ yòng Grammar Wiki xuéxí Zhōngwén.
I use the Grammar Wiki to study Chinese.

A: 你 怎么 上网?
Nǐ zěnme shàngwǎng?
How do you go online?

B: 我 用手机 上网。
Wǒ yòng shǒujī shàngwǎng.
I use my cell phone to go online.

A: 你 怎么 去北京?
Nǐ zěnme qù Běijīng?
How do you go to Beijing?

B: 我 坐火车 去。
Wǒ zuò huǒchē qù.
I take the train.

A: 你们 怎么 回家?
Nǐmen zěnme huíjiā?
How are you guys going to get home?

B: 我 开车 回家。
Wǒ kāichē huíjiā.
I'm driving home.

A: 你 [怎么] 买票?

Nǐ [zěnme] mǎi piào?

How do you buy tickets?

B: 我 [上网] 买票。

Wǒ [shàngwǎng] mǎi piào.

I go online to buy tickets.

Similar to

- Asking how something is with "zenmeyang" (HSK1), page 136
- Basic sentence order (HSK1), page 118
- How to do something with "zenme" (HSK1), page 112
- Asking why with "zenme" (HSK2)
- Simple rhetorical questions (HSK2)

Questions with "le ma"

Asking questions about completed actions will involve using both 了 (le) and 吗 (ma). These are simply added to the end of a sentence or statement. Just make sure that 了 (le) comes first, followed by 吗 (ma).

Basic Usage

Structure

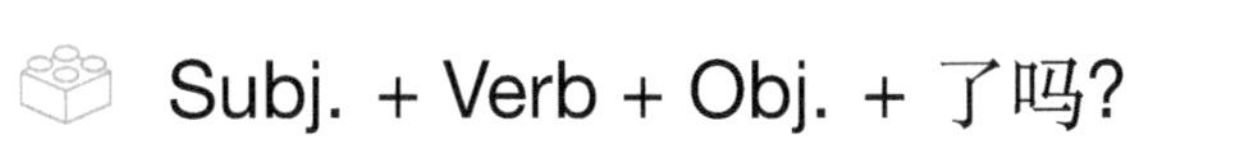

Note the order of 了 (le) and 吗 (ma).

Examples

- 你吃饭 了吗 ?
  Nǐ chīfàn le ma?
  Did you eat?
- 老板走 了吗 ?
  Lǎobǎn zǒu le ma?
  Did the boss leave?
- 你男朋友找到新工作 了吗 ?
  Nǐ nánpéngyou zhǎodào xīn gōngzuò le ma?
  Has your boyfriend found a new job yet?
- 妈妈，你昨天给我打电话 了吗 ?
  Māma, nǐ zuótiān gěi wǒ dǎ diànhuà le ma?
  Mom, did you call me yesterday?
- 你今天去上班 了吗 ?
  Nǐ jīntiān qù shàngbān le ma?
  Did you go to work today?

With a Topic

Structure

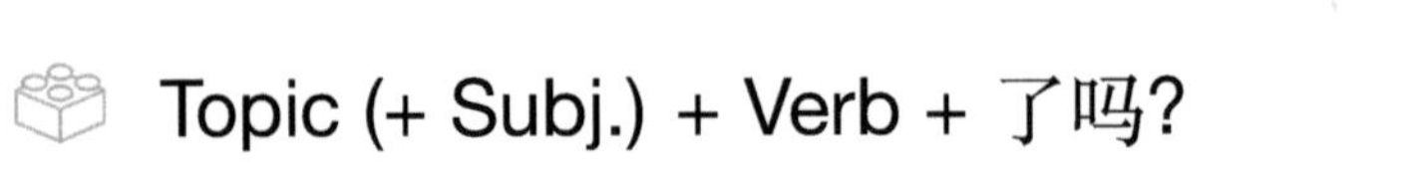

Topic (+ Subj.) + Verb + 了吗?

NOTE: in this structure, the topic is also the object for the verb.

Examples

- 晚饭你吃 了吗 ?
  Wǎnfàn nǐ chī le ma ?
  Did you eat dinner?
- 衣服你洗好 了吗 ?
  Yīfu nǐ xǐ hǎo le ma ?
  Have you finished washing the clothes?
- 作业你写完 了吗 ?
  Zuòyè nǐ xiě wán le ma ?
  Have you finishing doing homework?
- 这个电影你看 了吗 ?
  Zhège diànyǐng nǐ kàn le ma ?
  Have you seen this movie?
- 我的邮件你收到 了吗 ?
  Wǒ de yóujiàn nǐ shōudào le ma ?
  Have you received my email?

Finally, please note that this pattern is nothing more than the combination of the expressing completion with "le"[1] pattern and the yes/no questions with "ma"[2] pattern.

Similar to

- Yes-no questions with "ma" (HSK1), page 151
- Advanced yes-no questions with "ma" (HSK4)

1. Expressing completion with "le" (Grammar), page 70
2. Yes-no questions with "ma" (Grammar), page 151

Yes-no questions with “ma”

The question particle 吗 (ma) is a simple way to form questions in Chinese. By placing 吗 (ma) on the end of a statement, you convert it into a *yes/no question* (questions that could be answered with “yes” or “no” in English).

Basic Usage

Structure

Any statement can be converted into a yes/no question with 吗 (ma). You could think of 吗 (ma) as being like a question mark you say out loud. So the basic structure is:

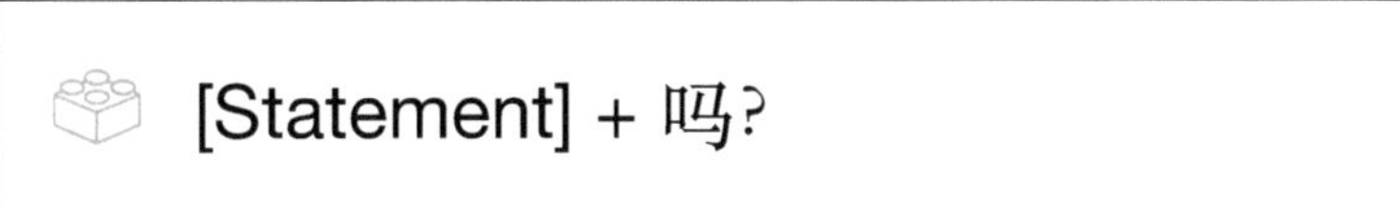

Examples

- 你喜欢咖啡。 *statement*

  Nǐ xǐhuan kāfēi.

  You like coffee.

The sentence “You like coffee” can easily be converted into the question “Do you like coffee?” by adding 吗 (ma):

- 你喜欢咖啡 吗 ? *question*

  Nǐ xǐhuan kāfēi ma ?

  Do you like coffee?

More examples of yes/no questions that revert to statements when you remove the 吗 (ma):

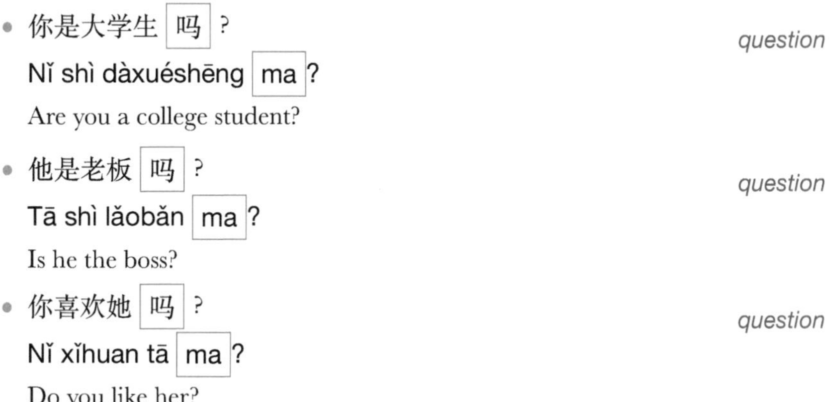

- 你是大学生 吗 ? *question*

  Nǐ shì dàxuéshēng ma ?

  Are you a college student?

- 他是老板 吗 ? *question*

  Tā shì lǎobǎn ma ?

  Is he the boss?

- 你喜欢她 吗 ? *question*

  Nǐ xǐhuan tā ma ?

  Do you like her?

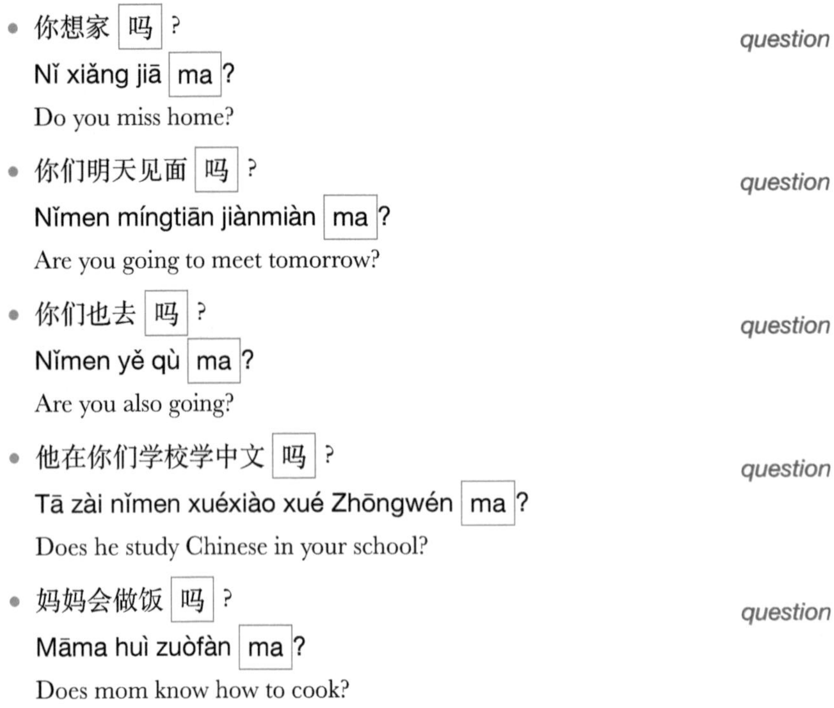

你想家 吗 ?
Nǐ xiǎng jiā ma?
Do you miss home?
question
你们明天见面 吗 ?
Nǐmen míngtiān jiànmiàn ma?
Are you going to meet tomorrow?
question
你们也去 吗 ?
Nǐmen yě qù ma?
Are you also going?
question
他在你们学校学中文 吗 ?
Tā zài nǐmen xuéxiào xué Zhōngwén ma?
Does he study Chinese in your school?
question
妈妈会做饭 吗 ?
Māma huì zuòfàn ma?
Does mom know how to cook?
question

It's important to remember that you do not normally add 吗 (ma) to a sentence that's *already a question*. For example:

✖ 你是谁 吗 ?
Nǐ shì shéi ma?
谁 (shéi) is a question word
✖ 这是不是书 吗 ?
Zhè shì bu shì shū ma?
是不是 (shì bu shì) is a question pattern

These would be something like "Are you who are you?" and "Is this is a book?" in English, both obviously ungrammatical. Still, if you're not careful, you may find yourself throwing a 吗 (ma) onto the end of a question that doesn't need it. Many learners make this mistake, so don't worry if it happens every once in a while, just catch it and remember it the next time.

How to Answer

You can answer a Chinese yes-no question in one of two ways:

- Answer with 对 (duì) or the more casual 嗯 (ǹg) to affirm what was asked.
- Answer a clearer "yes" by simply repeating the positive form of the verb, or "no" by using the negative form of the verb.

Here's the slightly tricky part: if you answer with 对 (duì) and the question is in the *positive*, then you're saying **"yes"** (and affirming the *positive* verb in the question). If you answer with 对 (duì) and the question is in the *negative*, then you're saying "**no**" (and affirming the *negative* verb in the question). Let's take a look at some examples of this sort.

A: 你是大学生 吗 ?
Nǐ shì dàxuéshēng ma ?
Are you a college student?

Positive verb in the question

B: 对。
Duì.
Yes, I am.

对 (duì) affirms the positive verb.

A: 你 没有 工作 吗 ?
Nǐ méiyǒu gōngzuò ma ?
Do you not have a job?

Negative verb in the question

B: 对。
Duì.
No, I don't.

对 (duì) affirms the negative verb.

Now let's try some answers that reuse the verb for a super-clear "yes" or "no," which works the same way regardless of whether it's a positive or a negative verb in the question.

A: 你明天 不来 吗 ?
Nǐ míngtiān bù lái ma ?
You're not coming tomorrow?

Negative verb in the question

B: 来。
Lái.
Yes, I'll come.

Repeat the verb for greater clarity.

A: 你明天 不来 吗 ?
Nǐ míngtiān bù lái ma ?
You're not coming tomorrow?

Negative verb in the question

B: 不来。
Bù lái.
No, I won't come.

The negative verb means "no."

Finally, a mix of the two ways to answer, where one person is asking questions of two different people.

A: 你喜欢中国菜 吗 ?
Nǐ xǐhuan Zhōngguó cài ma ?
Do you like Chinese food?

Positive verb in the question

B: 喜欢。 *Repeat the verb for greater clarity.*

Xǐhuan.

Yes, I do.

A: 你 不喜欢 中国菜 吗 ? *Negative verb in the question*

Nǐ bù xǐhuan Zhōngguó cài ma ?

Don't you like Chinese food?

- **C:** 对。 *对 (duì) affirms the negative verb.*

Duì.

No. (I don't.)

You sometimes hear that “yes” in Chinese is 是 (shì) and “no” is 不是 (bù shì). This can be true, but *only when the main verb in the question is also 是 (shì)*. If the verb in the question is something else, like 喜欢 (xǐhuan), then that verb becomes the word for “yes.” It's been said that Chinese has hundreds of ways to say “yes,” and this is why: *every verb can be used to mean “yes.”*

More Advanced Usage

However, this doesn't mean that a sentence *can't ever* have a question word and 吗 (ma). If a sentence contains verbs of understanding such as 知道 (zhīdào), 了解 (liǎojiě), 明白 (míngbai), 认识 (rènshi), etc., then 吗 (ma) can still be added at the end of the question. You will later learn more about these advanced yes-no questions with “ma”.

Similar to

- Placement of question words (HSK1), page 138
- Simple rhetorical questions (HSK2)

The “shi… de” construction for emphasizing details

Also known as: 是……的结构 (shì… de jiégòu), 是……的 sentence and 是……的 pattern.

The 是……的 (shì… de) construction is used to draw attention to certain information in a sentence. It's often used to ask questions that seek specific information, or to explain a situation by emphasizing a particular detail. While not strictly tied to any “tense,” the 是……的 construction is frequently used when asking or telling *details* about the past.

This use of 是……的 (shì… de) is usually emphasized in textbooks over other uses, and therefore is sometimes called the “classic” 是……的 construction.

When to Use It

Even if you understand that 了 is not used to mark “past tense” in Chinese, it's possible that you incorrectly use it that way sometimes. For example, what if you want to ask a question about something that happened in the past? Would you ever say one of the following sentences?

✘ 你昨天 几点 到 了？

Nǐ zuótiān jǐ diǎn dào le?

What time did you arrive yesterday?

✘ 你跟 谁 去 了？

Nǐ gēn shéi qù le?

Who did you go with?

✘ 他 用什么 打你 了？

Tā yòng shénme dǎ nǐ le?

What did he use to hit you?

In each of these sentences above, 了 is not the right choice, because you're not asking if an event happened or not. You're asking about details of past events. When you are singling out details for emphasis–in a question or a statement–you need to use the 是……的 construction.

A 是……的 construction can pick out any detail that's related to a past event. Whatever comes immediately after 是 is emphasized. Check out this example:

A: 昨天我去杭州了。

Zuótiān wǒ qù Hángzhōu le.

I went to Hangzhou yesterday.

B: 你 是 怎么 去 的 ？
Nǐ shì zěnme qù de?
How did you get there?

A: 我 是 坐火车 去 的 。
Wǒ shì zuò huǒchē qù de.
I went by train.

Now let's revisit those other three sentences and ask the questions correctly with 是……的:

✔ 你昨天 是 几点 到 的 ？
Nǐ zuótiān shì jǐ diǎn dào de?
What time did you arrive yesterday?

✔ 你 是 跟谁 去 的 ？
Nǐ shì gēn shéi qù de?
Who did you go with?

✔ 他 是 用什么 打你 的 ？
Tā shì yòng shénme dǎ nǐ de?
What did he use to hit you?

Affirmative Form

是……的 is not generally used for reporting new information but for adding important details that make the information clearer. You could think of 是……的 as being equivalent to saying one of the following in English:

- "The situation is that…"
- "It's that… "
- "It was… that… "

Structure

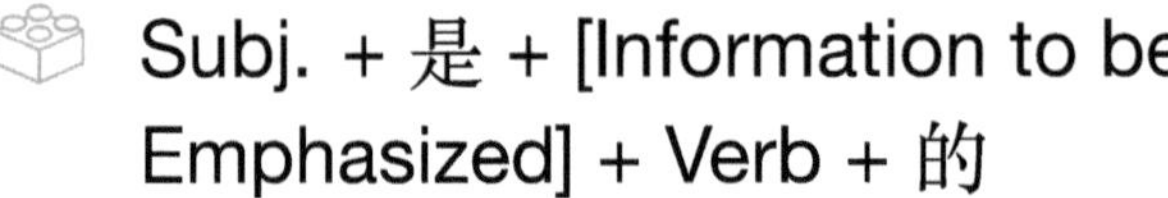

Subj. + 是 + [Information to be Emphasized] + Verb + 的

This structure can be used to emphasize any detail, but most commonly it emphasizes **time**, **manner**, or **place**. Don't worry if this still seems a little confusing; lots of helpful examples are coming up!

Examples

A: 你们 是 什么时候 到 的 ? — *Emphasizing "when"*
Nǐmen shì shénme shíhou dào de?
When did you guys arrive?

B: 我们 是 昨天 到 的 。 — *"Yesterday" is emphasized.*
Wǒmen shì zuótiān dào de.
We arrived yesterday.

A: 你 是 在哪儿 出生 的 ? — *"Where" is emphasized.*
Nǐ shì zài nǎr chūshēng de?
Where were you born?

B: 我 是 在香港 出生 的 。 — *"In Hong Kong" is emphasized.*
Wǒ shì zài Xiānggǎng chūshēng de.
I was born in Hong Kong.

Although this structure is called the 是……的 construction, the 是 is nearly always optional. You will often hear this structure with 是 omitted, so be aware. The only time 是 is required in this construction is when it's being negated. Other than that, 是 is commonly omitted.

A: 你 骑自行车 来 的 吗? — *Emphasizing "by bike"*
Nǐ qí zìxíngchē lái de ma?
Did you come by bike?

B: 我 走 来 的 。 — *Emphasizing "by foot"*
Wǒ zǒu lái de.
I came by foot.

A: 谁 告诉你 的 ? — *Emphasizing "who"*
Shéi gàosu nǐ de?
Who told you?

B: 一个同事 告诉我 的 。 — *Emphasizing "a colleague"*
Yī gè tóngshì gàosu wǒ de.
A colleague told me.

You might be wondering, "can I still say the same thing without the 是 and the 的?" The answer is that in most cases, *no, not really*. While the 是 can sometimes be dropped, these examples sound weird without the 的. It's just a part of learning to ask questions naturally in Mandarin. You don't have to learn a "past tense," but you do have to learn this way of asking for details about the past sooner or later.

Negative Form

是…… 的 sentences can only be negated with 不, as 没 can not be used to negate 是. Remember that you need *both* the 不 *and* the 是 together to make the correct negative form.

Some examples:

✔ 他们 不是 在网上 认识 的 。
Tāmen bù shì zài wǎngshàng rènshi de.
They didn't meet online.

✔ 他 不是 跟我们一起 去 的 。
Tā bù shì gēn wǒmen yīqǐ qù de.
He didn't go with us.

✘ 我 不 坐地铁 来 的 。
Wǒ bù zuò dìtiě lái de.
I didn't come by metro.
The 是 is missing

✘ 我 不 在中国 出生 的 。
Wǒ bù zài Zhōngguó chūshēng de.
I wasn't born in China.
The 是 is missing

Note that negating a 是…… 的 construction creates the implication that the action in the sentence *was* carried out, and only the detail emphasized by 是…… 的 is being denied. So, in the second sentence, the implication is that 他 didn't go with 我们, but *did* go out with *someone*. So negative 是…… 的 constructions would work nicely in the final scenes of detective dramas.

Used in a Question

是…… 的 constructions can be made into questions in the usual three ways to form questions in Chinese:

- With a question particle
- Within affirmative-negative questions
- With a question word

Some examples:

- 她 用邮件 回复 的 吗?
Tā yòng yóujiàn huífù de ma?
Did she reply by email?
吗 is a question particle

- 你们 是不是 去年 认识 的 ？
  Nǐmen shì bu shì qùnián rènshi de?
  Did you meet each other last year?

  是不是 is an affirmative-negative pattern

- 这个东西 多少钱 买 的 ？
  Zhège dōngxi duōshao qián mǎi de?
  How much did you buy this thing for?

  多少 is a question word

Is 是 always optional?

Generally, 是 can be omitted, and the meaning will not change. However, in a small number of cases, omitting 是 will make it unclear which part of the sentence is being emphasized. In these cases, 是 clearly indicates which words are being emphasized. Take a look at this example:

- 你上周和他去北京 的 吗?
  Nǐ shàng zhōu hé tā qù Běijīng de ma?
  Did you go to Beijing with him last weekend?

This sentence could emphasize 上周 (time), or 和他 (part of the subject). A simple 是 can make clear which one the speaker is emphasizing.

✔ 你 是 上周 和他去北京 的 吗?
Nǐ shì shàng zhōu hé tā qù Běijīng de ma?
Was it last week that you went to Beijing with him?

上周 is emphasized

✔ 你上周 是 和他 去北京 的 吗?
Nǐ shàng zhōu shì hé tā qù Běijīng de ma?
Was it him that you went to Beijing with last week?

和他 is emphasized

Position of 的

Until now we've said that the 的 appears at the end of the sentence in a 是……的 construction. This is very often the case. However, it can actually appear in one of two places. Take a look at the examples below:

✔ 我们 是 用 Skype 开 会 的 。
Wǒmen shì yòng Skype kāi huì de.
We had a meeting by Skype.

✔ 我们 是 用 Skype 开 的 会 。
Wǒmen shì yòng Skype kāi de huì.
We had a meeting by Skype.

As you can see, when the verb is followed by an object, 的 can go before *or* after the object. Both sentences are grammatically correct, but the first the sentence could be referring to either a specific event in the past or habitual actions.

Take a look at these two sentences which remove the ambiguity by including a bit more information about the timeframe:

- 那次 我们 是 用 Skype 开 会 的。
  Nà cì wǒmen shì yòng Skype kāi huì de.
  That time we had the meeting by Skype.
- 我们 平时 是 用 Skype 开 会 的。
  Wǒmen píngshí shì yòng Skype kāi huì de.
  We usually have meetings by Skype.

For the most part, you should be fine regularly putting 的 at the end of your 是……的 sentences. Just be aware that there is some potential for ambiguity in certain situations. If you don't want to move 的 around, then including a bit of extra information about time can keep things clear.

Completed Action

It's important to note that while the 是……的 construction also indicates that an action has been completed, this is not the *purpose* of a 是……的 construction. The completed action part is more like a *prerequisite* for using 是……的. This means you shouldn't use 是……的 just to indicate that an action is completed. Use the aspect particle 了 for that. Instead, use 是…… 的 to draw attention to certain details of a completed action.

Similar to

- The "shi... de" construction for indicating purpose (HSK2)
- The "shi... de" patterns: an overview (HSK2)
- Using "de" (modal particle) (HSK4)

Comparing "bu" and "mei"

Both 不 (bù) and 没 (méi) can be placed in front of a verb or adjective to negate its meaning. However, 不 (bù) and 没 (méi) are not usually interchangeable, so it's important to learn when you must use 不 (bù) as opposed to 没 (méi), and vice versa.

不 (bù) Negates in the Present and Future

不 (bù) is generally used to negate an action that you *do not want to do* or *do not intend to do* (in the future). So expressing things like "I don't want to go" or "I'm not going" would be uses of 不 (bù).

Structure

Subj. + 不 + Verb

Examples

Whether it's "don't wanna do it" or "not gonna do it," use 不 (bù):

- 我今天晚上 不 喝酒。
  Wǒ jīntiān wǎnshang bù hējiǔ.
  Tonight I'm not going to drink.
- 爸爸 不 回来吃晚饭。
  Bàba bù huílái chī wǎnfàn.
  Dad is not coming back to eat dinner.
- 老板明天 不 来。
  Lǎobǎn míngtiān bù lái.
  The boss won't come tomorrow.
- 我知道这个周末 不 下雨。
  Wǒ zhīdào zhège zhōumò bù xiàyǔ.
  I know it's not going to rain this weekend.
- 你女朋友 不 跟你一起去吗?
  Nǐ nǚpéngyou bù gēn nǐ yīqǐ qù ma?
  Is your girlfriend not going with you?

不 (bù) Negates Habitual Actions

不 (bù) can be used to negate habitual actions, to express what you just aren't in the habit of doing, such as eating meat, or watching TV, or drinking alcohol. This is simply done by placing 不 (bù) in front of the verb.

Structure

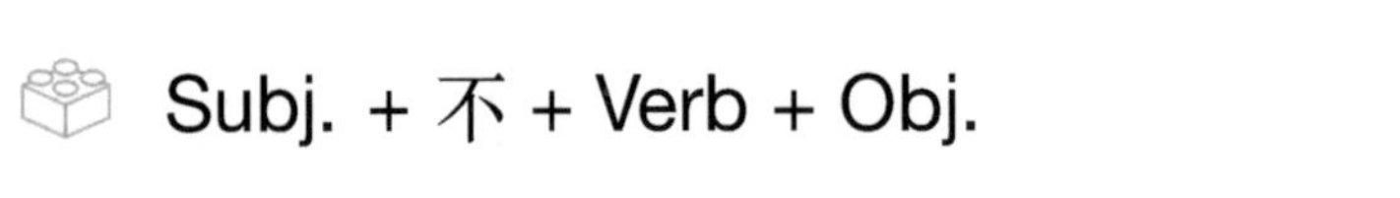

Subj. + 不 + Verb + Obj.

Examples

- 我 不 吃肉。
  Wǒ bù chī ròu.
  I don't eat meat.
- 你们都 不 喝酒吗?
  Nǐmen dōu bù hējiǔ ma?
  Do you all not drink alcohol?
- 他 不 喜欢说话。
  Tā bù xǐhuan shuōhuà.
  He doesn't like to speak.
- 你 不 用手机看书吗?
  Nǐ bù yòng shǒujī kàn shū ma?
  Do you not use your phone to read books?
- 你晚上 不 洗澡吗?
  Nǐ wǎnshang bù xǐzǎo ma?
  Don't you shower at night?

Please note that, while it is grammatically correct to use 没 (méi) in all the sentences above, 没 (méi) does not negate any *habitual* actions. The sentences above, if they contained 没 (méi) instead of 不 (bù), would express that the speaker *didn't do* the named activity (at one particular point *in the past*). So it would not be about *habitual actions*.

不 (bù) is Normally Used with Adjectives

When it comes to a simple negation of an adjective (such as "not cold"), use 不 (bù).

Structure

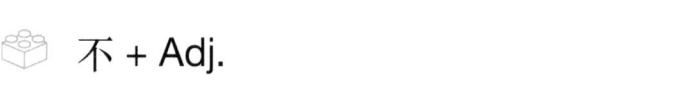

Examples

- 我们 不 饿。
  Wǒmen bù è.
  We're not hungry.
- 你 不 胖。
  Nǐ bù pàng.
  You are not fat.
- 我家 不 远。
  Wǒ jiā bù yuǎn.
  My home is not far.
- 今天 不 冷。
  Jīntiān bù lěng.
  Today it isn't cold.
- 我觉得 Starbucks 的咖啡 不 好喝。
  Wǒ juéde Starbucks de kāfēi bù hǎohē.
  I think the coffee at Starbucks isn't good.

不 (bù) is for Asking Questions

There are couple ways to use 不 (bù) to ask questions. One such way is through affirmative-negative questions. This is done by stating a verb and then immediately repeating that verb in a negative state (with 不 (bù)).

Structure

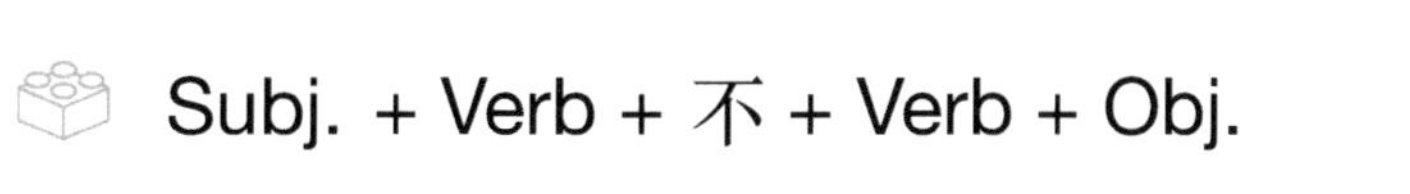

Examples

- 你是不 是 我的老师？
  Nǐ shì bu shì wǒ de lǎoshī?
  Are you my teacher or not?
- 她想 不 想来？
  Tā xiǎng bu xiǎnglái?
  Does she want to come?
- 你爱 不 爱我？
  Nǐ ài bu ài wǒ?
  Do you love me or not?
- 你们周末上 不 上班？
  Nǐmen zhōumò shàng bu shàngbān?
  Do you all go to work on weekends?
- 你的外国朋友们喜 不 喜欢吃中国菜？
  Nǐ de wàiguó péngyoumen xǐ bu xǐhuan chī Zhōngguó cài?
  Do your foreign friends like to eat Chinese food?

不 (bù) can also be used to form tag questions. Tag questions use the positive-negative question form, but are placed at the end of the sentence. Tag questions are used to seek approval or acceptance for a statement, very similar to the English "OK?" or "right?" You can't use 没 (méi) for this.

✘ 我们去吃饭，好 没 好？
Wǒmen qù chīfàn, hǎo méi hǎo?

✔ 我们去吃饭，好 不 好？
Wǒmen qù chīfàn, hǎo bu hǎo?
Let's go eat, is that OK?

✘ 你们是好朋友，对 没 对？
Nǐmen shì hǎo péngyou, duì méi duì?

✔ 你们是好朋友，对 不 对？
Nǐmen shì hǎo péngyou, duì bu duì?
You are good friends, right?

没 (méi) Negates Past Actions

没 (méi) and 没有 (méiyǒu) can both be used to negate actions that occurred in the past[1], or to say that something has not happened yet.

Structure

Subj. + 没 (有) + Verb + Obj.

Examples

- ✔ 他 没有 打电话给我。
  Tā méiyǒu dǎ diànhuà gěi wǒ.
  He did not give me a call.
- ✔ 你 没 去上班吗?
  Nǐ méi qù shàngbān ma?
  You didn't go to work?
- ✔ 我昨天 没 喝酒。
  Wǒ zuótiān méi hējiǔ.
  I did not drink alcohol yesterday.
- ✔ 妈妈 没有 做晚饭。
  Māma méiyǒu zuò wǎnfàn.
  Mom did not cook dinner.
- ✔ 他们吃完饭以后 没 付钱。
  Tāmen chī wán fàn yǐhòu méi fù qián.
  They didn't pay after they finished eating.
- ✘ 我昨天 不 喝酒。
  Wǒ zuótiān bù hējiǔ.
  I not drink wine yesterday.
- ✘ 我上个周末 不 跟他见面。
  Wǒ shàng gè zhōumò bù gēn tā jiànmiàn.
  I not meet with him last weekend.
- ✘ 上个月你 不 去北京吗?
  Shàng gè yuè nǐ bù qù Běijīng?
  You not go to Beijing last month?

---

1. Negation of past actions with “meiyou” (Grammar), page 116

There are a few things worth noting in these examples. For one, it is still grammatically correct to leave out the 有 (yǒu) in the sentences using 没有 (méiyǒu). Also, the sentences using 不 (bù) *would be* grammatically correct, if not for the time words telling us that it is definitely the **past** we're talking about.

Only 没 (méi) Negates 有 (yǒu)

没 (méi) can be used to negate the verb 有 (yǒu)[1] ("to have") to mean "do not have." You can only use 没 (méi) to convey this meaning. It is grammatically incorrect to use 不 (bù) to negate 有 (yǒu).

Structure

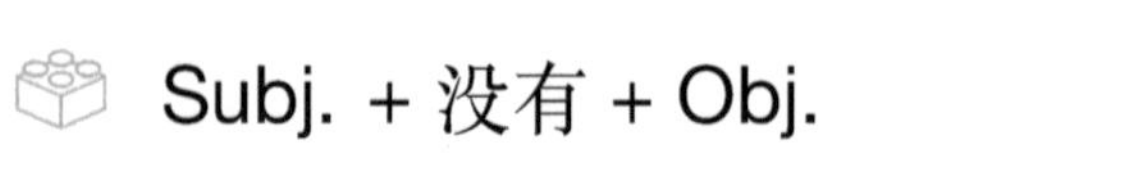
Subj. + 没有 + Obj.

Examples

- ✘ 我 不有 钱。
  Wǒ bù yǒu qián.
- ✔ 我 没有 钱。
  Wǒ méiyǒu qián.
  I don't have money.
- ✘ 他 不有 女朋友。
  Tā bù yǒu nǚpéngyou.
- ✔ 他 没有 女朋友。
  Tā méiyǒu nǚpéngyou.
  He doesn't have a girlfriend.

There are times when you can leave out 有 (yǒu) entirely while still expressing 没有 (méiyǒu), (meaning "to not have" or "there is no"). One well-known example of this is 没办法 (méi bànfǎ) ("there is no way" [that's gonna happen]). Both 没 (méi) and 没有 (méiyǒu) are correct, however.

- 我 没 办法。
  Wǒ méi bànfǎ.
  I don't have a way.

---

1. Negation of past actions with "meiyou" (Grammar), page 116

- 我 没有 办法。
  Wǒ méiyǒu bànfǎ.
  I don't have a way.

(You can also use 没办法 (méi bànfǎ) to express other meanings.)

没 (méi) is for Making Comparisons

没 (méi) or 没有 (méiyǒu) can be used to make simple comparisons meaning "not as… as…":

Structure

Noun 1 + 没有 + Noun 2 + Adj.

Examples

✘ 你 不有 我高。
Nǐ bù yǒu wǒ gāo.

✔ 你 没有 我高。
Nǐ méiyǒu wǒ gāo.
You are not as tall as me.

✘ 我的手机 不有 他的手机贵。
Wǒ de shǒujī bù yǒu tā de shǒujī guì.

✔ 我的手机 没有 他的手机贵。
Wǒ de shǒujī méiyǒu tā de shǒujī guì.
My cell phone isn't as expensive as his.

✘ 我们都 不有 老板忙。
Wǒmen dōu bù yǒu lǎobǎn máng.

✔ 我们都 没有 老板忙。
Wǒmen dōu méiyǒu lǎobǎn máng.
We all are not as busy as the boss.

✘ 上海的冬天 不有 北京的冬天冷。
Shànghǎi de dōngtiān bù yǒu Běijīng de dōngtiān lěng.

✔ 上海的冬天 没有 北京的冬天冷。

Shànghǎi de dōngtiān méiyǒu Běijīng de dōngtiān lěng.

Shanghai winters are not as cold Beijing winters.

You can only use 没 (méi) or 没有 (méiyǒu) for this purpose, and **not** 不 (bù).

不 (bù) is Used Almost Exclusively with Certain Verbs

Certain verbs just don't get negated by 没 (méi) or 没有 (méiyǒu) ever. These include the verbs 是 (shì) ("to be") and 在 (zài) ("to be (in a place)"), as well as some psychological verbs such as 知道 (zhīdào) ("to know") and 认识 (rènshi) ("to know (a person)"). For these verbs, it's best to just take them on a case-by-case basis. Being aware of their existence can save you a fair bit of confusion.

✘ 他以前 没 是我的老板。

Tā yǐqián méi shì wǒ de lǎobǎn.

✔ 他以前 不 是我的老板。

Tā yǐqián bù shì wǒ de lǎobǎn.

He was not my boss before.

✘ 我 没 知道他要来。

Wǒ méi zhīdào tā yào lái.

✔ 我 不 知道他要来。

Wǒ bù zhīdào tā yào lái.

I didn't know he was coming.

✘ 他小时候 没 认识她。

Tā xiǎo shíhou méi rènshi tā.

✔ 他小时候 不 认识她。

Tā xiǎo shíhou bù rènshi tā.

He did not know her when he was young.

⚠ 昨天我 没 在家。

Zuótiān wǒ méi zài jiā.

Use of 没 with 在 is technically incorrect, but you sometimes hear it.

✔ 昨天我 不 在家。

Zuótiān wǒ bù zài jiā.

I was not home yesterday.

Note that in non-standard Mandarin you might encounter exceptions to this rule. It's still useful to know the rule!

Similar to

- Negation of "you" with "mei" (HSK1), page 15
- Negation of past actions with "meiyou" (HSK1), page 116
- Standard negation with "bu" (HSK1), page 18
- Affirmative-negative question (HSK2)
- Tag questions with "bu" (HSK2)
- Basic comparisons with "meiyou" (HSK3)

Keyword Index

Look up grammar points based on keywords they contain.

啊 (a), 79

吧 (ba), 82, 84
八 (bā), 50
百 (bǎi), 50
不 (bù), 18, 30, 161

的 (de), 68, 74, 155
点 (diǎn), 56, 60
点钟 (diǎnzhōng), 56, 60
都 (dōu), 21
多 (duō), 28

二 (èr), 50

个 (gè), 42

号 (hào), 45
和 (hé), 32
很 (hěn), 126
后 (hòu), 34
会 (huì), 102, 106

几 (jǐ), 134
角 (jiǎo), 131
叫 (jiào), 97
九 (jiǔ), 50

块 (kuài), 131

来 (lái), 86
了 (le), 63, 66, 70, 124, 149
礼拜 (lǐbài), 47
六 (liù), 50

吗 (ma), 149, 151
毛 (máo), 131
没 (méi), 15, 116, 161
没有 (méiyǒu), 15, 116, 161

哪儿 (nǎér), 138
呢 (ne), 76
能 (néng), 109
年 (nián), 45

七 (qī), 50
千 (qiān), 50
前 (qián), 36
请 (qǐng), 94
去 (qù), 86, 99

日 (rì), 45

三 (sān), 50
谁 (shéi), 138
什么 (shénme), 138
什么时候 (shénmeshíhòu), 138
十 (shí), 50
是 (shì), 121, 155
四 (sì), 50
岁 (suì), 40

太 (tài), 30, 124

为什么 (wèishénme), 138
五 (wǔ), 50

想 (xiǎng), 104
些 (xiē), 129
星期 (xīngqī), 47

也 (yě), 23
一 (yī), 50
一些 (yīxiē), 129
以 (yǐ), 34, 36
以后 (yǐhòu), 34
以前 (yǐqián), 36
有 (yǒu), 15, 90, 92
元 (yuán), 131
月 (yuè), 45

在 (zài), 13, 88, 114
怎么 (zěnme), 112, 136, 138
怎么样 (zěnmeyàng), 136
正 (zhèng), 13
正在 (zhèngzài), 13
周 (zhōu), 47

Glossary

We strive to avoid unnecessarily technical terms on the Chinese Grammar Wiki, but occasionally it's sort of necessary, and sometimes even useful (yes, really!). So to help you out, we've placed all of the grammatical terms related to Mandarin Chinese in one place. Each term has a page on the wiki with a more complete description, and many pages also have lists of grammar points related to the term.

List of Mandarin Grammar Terms

Action verb — *Also known as: 动作动词 (dòngzuò dòngcí) and 行为动词 (xíngwéi dòngcí).* Action verbs describe what a subject did, is doing, or will do, physically.

Adjective — *Also known as: 形容词 (xíngróngcí).* Adjectives are the "describing" words of a language. In Chinese, they have some characteristics that they don't have in English.

Adjectival phrase — *Also known as: 形容词性词组 (xíngróngcí-xìng duǎnyǔ) and adjective phrase.* Adjectival phrases often consist of just an adjective and the adverbs modifying it, but they might also have other structures, such as an adjective and complement.

Adjectival predicate sentence — *Also known as: 形容词谓语句 (xíngróngcí wèiyǔ jù) and 形容词性谓语句 (xíngróngcí-xìng wèiyǔ jù).* A fancy name for a sentence where the predicate consists of an adjective.

Adverb — *Also known as: 副词 (fùcí).* Adverbs are words that modify verbs and adjectives. In Chinese, word order of adverbs is much stricter than in English. Chinese adverbs normally come before the main verb of a sentence, but in some cases come right at the beginning of a sentence.

Adverbial — *Also known as: 状语 (zhuàngyǔ).* An adverbial is a sentence element that functions like an adverb, modifying a verb or adjective.

Adverbial phrase — *Also known as: 副词短语 (fùcí duǎnyǔ) and adverb phrase.* An adverbial phrase is a phrase with two or more words that act like an adverb, modifying a verb or adjective.

Affirmative-negative question — *Also known as: 正反问句 (zhèng-fǎn wènjù) and alternative questions.* A common way to form questions in Chinese is to first use a verb in the positive, then repeat the same verb in its negative form, similar to how in English we can say, "Do you have money or not?" or "Have you or have you not been to the park?" This sentence pattern feels a lot more natural in Chinese than those admittedly awkward English equivalents, however.

Affix — *Also known as: 词缀 (cízhuì).* An affix is a linguistic unit added to the beginning, middle or end of a word to change its meaning (e.g. prefix, infix, suffix).

Aspect — *Also known as: 动作状态 (dòngzuò zhuàngtài).* Chinese does not use the concept of formal tenses. Instead, it employs what is called "grammatical aspect." Rather than conjugating its verbs, Chinese uses particles to indicate how a verb works within a particular timeframe, or how the verb relates to the flow of time. The particles most often used to indicate aspect in Chinese are 了 (le), 过 (guo), and 着 (zhe).

Aspectual particle — *Also known as: 动态助词 (dòngtài zhùcí).* These words are added to verbs to indicate aspect (not the same as tense). The particles most often used to indicate aspect in Chinese are 了 (le), 过 (guo), and 着 (zhe).

Attributive — *Also known as: 定语 (dìngyǔ).* An attributive is the word or phrase that directly precedes the noun it describes. Frequently it is linked to the noun with the structural particle 的 (de).

Auxiliary verb — *Also known as: modal verb, 助动词 (zhùdòngcí), 情态动词 (qíngtài dòngcí) and 能愿动词 (néngyuàn dòngcí).* Auxiliary verbs are "helping" verbs that come before main verbs and help express a tone or mood. (The word "modal" comes from "mood.") In English, auxiliary verbs include words like "should," "will," and "can," which all change something about the situation and the speaker's attitude. Auxiliary verbs express capability, possibility, necessity, obligation or willingness.

Cardinal number — *Also known as: 基数词 (jīshùcí).* Cardinal numbers are numbers such as 1, 2, or 3 used to indicate quantity. They contrast with ordinal numbers.

Causative verb — *Also known as: 使令动词 (shǐlìng dòngcí) and 使役动词 (shǐyì dòngcí).* A causative verb is a kind of verb that is used to indicate that someone or something causes something else to do or be something. In Chinese, 让 (ràng) is a major player in this space.

Complement — *Also known as: 补语 (bǔyǔ) and objective complement.* A complement is a word or phrase following a verb (or sometimes an adjective) that provides additional meaning to the verb phrase. Complements are not the same as objects, and can be as short as one character, or practically as long as a sentence. Complements provide additional information associated with verbs, such as degree, result, direction or possibility, and are extremely common. Complements are not a form of flattery (those are compliments); they're much more versatile than that!

Complex sentence — *Also known as: 复句 (fùjù).* A complex sentence is a sentence with one main clause and one or more subordinate clauses.

Conjunction — *Also known as: 连词 (liáncí).* Conjunctions in Chinese do exactly what they do in English: connect things. They help make the transition between ideas smoother and also show the relationships between those ideas.

Content word — *Also known as: 实词 (shící).* Content words refer to real objects in the real world, whether solid and palpable, or observable in some other way. These words refer to objects, actions, concepts, and even emotions, which exist in some real way as more than just grammatical tools. Words that serve purely grammatical roles are called function words.

Coverb — *Also known as: 副动词 (fùdòngcí) and 伴动词 (bàndòngcí).* A coverb is a verb that modifies the main verb of a sentence when used with its own object.

Degree adverb — *Also known as: 程度副词 (chéngdù fùcí) and adverb of degree.* Degree adverbs intensify or in some other way modify the degree of expression of the adjective (or verb).

Degree complement — *Also known as: 程度补语 (chéngdù bǔyǔ) and complement of degree.* While most complements follow verbs, degree complements can follow both verbs and adjectives. These complements intensify or modify the degree of expression of the verb or adjective.

Demonstrative pronoun — *Also known as: 指示代词 (zhǐshì dàicí).* A demonstrative pronoun is a pronoun used in the place of a noun and specifies what is being referred to.

Dependent clause — *Also known as: 从句 (cóngjù).* A dependent clause is dependent on and modifies an independent clause. Dependent clauses have a subject and verb, but also start with a subordinate conjunction, making it clear that they are not meant to stand on their own.

Direct object — *Also known as: 直接宾语 (zhíjiē bīnyǔ).* A direct object is what is being acted upon, thus receiving the action of a verb. In Chinese grammar, direct objects are often simply referred to as "objects."

Direction complement — *Also known as: 趋向补语 (qūxiàng bǔyǔ), directional complement and complement of direction.* A direction complement is a complement used to describe the direction of a verb. Verbs often already have some inherent movement implied, but by adding a direction complement, it becomes clearer where, exactly, that action is going.

Directional verb — *Also known as: 趋向动词 (qūxiàng dòngcí).* Directional verbs can be added to other verbs in a direction complement, illustrating which direction the verb is going.

Directional complement — See **direction complement**

Distinguishing word — *Also known as: 区别词 (qūbiécí) and attributive adjective.* "Distinguishing words" are rather foreign to the English speaker. On the surface they may seem like regular adjectives, but distinguishing words cannot have degree, so they cannot be modified by adverbs. Unlike normal adjectives, sentences involving distinguishing words use 是 (shì), and usually 的 (de) as well. Common words include the Chinese words for "male," "female," "real," "fake," and colors.

Existential verb — *Also known as: 存现动词 (cúnxiàn dòngcí).* Existential verbs declare the existence or nonexistence of things.

Function word — *Also known as: 虚词 (xūcí).* Function words do not refer to real objects in the real world; rather they serve purely grammatical roles in sentences, drawing relationships and logical connections between the content words in a sentence. Words that refer to real objects in the real world are called content words.

Judgment verb — *Also known as: 关系动词 (guānxì dòngcí) and 判断动词 (pànduàn dòngcí).* Judgment verbs are verbs used to express the speaker's judgment. This can be as simple as the verb "to be," but also covers a wide range of other verbs.

Indirect object — *Also known as: 间接宾语 (jiànjiē bīnyǔ).* Indirect objects occur when there are two objects in a sentence. The indirect object is for/to whom/what the action of the verb is done and who/what is receiving the direct object. In Chinese grammar, indirect objects are often referred to as second objects.

Independent clause — *Also known as: 主句 (zhǔjù).* An independent clause is a clause that has a subject and a predicate that modifies the subject, allowing it to stand alone as a sentence.

Independent phrase — *Also known as: 独立语 (dúlì yǔ).* An independent phrase has no subject acting out the verb in the sentence.

Interjection — *Also known as: 叹词 (tàncí) and 感叹词 (gǎntàncí).* This type of word is used in exclamations or various kinds of emotional response.

Interrogative pronoun — See **question word**

Intransitive verb — *Also known as: 不及物动词 (bùjíwù dòngcí).* Intransitive verbs are verbs which take no direct object.

Location word — *Also known as: 方位名词 (fāngwèi míngcí), 方位词 (fāngwèi cí) and noun of locality.* Location words are nouns showing direction and location.

Main clause — See **independent clause**

Measure word — *Also known as: 量词 (liàngcí) and classifier.* Measure words are used together with numerals to indicate the quantity of a noun, and sometimes even of an action. The general term for "measure word" in linguistics is "classifier," because measure words involve some kind of classification of the noun (or action) being counted.

Mimetic word — See **onomatopoeia**

Modal adverb — *Also known as: 语气副词 (yǔqì fùcí) and tone adverb.* Modal adverbs express likelihood with adverbs such as probably, possibly, evidently, certainly, etc.

Modal particle — *Also known as: 语气助词 (yǔqì zhùcí), 语气词 (yǔqì cí), Sentence-final particle and Sentential particle.* Modal particles are words used at the end of sentences to indicate mood, or attitude. They tend to be neutral tone and hard to translate, but they add a bit of "flavor" to a sentence. See also particles.

Modal verb — See **auxiliary verb**

Negative adverb — *Also known as: 否定副词 (fǒudìng fùcí).* Negative adverbs negate verbs and adjectives to make a negative statement. The main ones in Chinese are 不 (bù) and 没 (méi).

Noun — *Also known as: 名词 (míngcí).* You may have learned these as "person, place, or thing." Nouns often act as subjects, are modified by adjectives, and can be counted with measure words in Chinese.

Noun measure word — *Also known as: 名量词 (míngliàngcí) and nominal measure word.* As the name suggests, these are measure words that are only used for nouns.

Noun phrase — *Also known as: 名词性短语 (míngcí-xìng duǎnyǔ).* A noun phrase is a phrase with a noun or pronoun as a head word that has any sort of modifier.

Numeral — *Also known as: 数词 (shùcí).* A numeral is a symbol that represents a number.

Nominal predicate sentence — *Also known as: 名词谓语句 (míngcí wèiyǔjù).* Nominal predicate sentences are sentences with a noun phrase that functions as the main predicate of the sentence.

Object — *Also known as: 宾语 (bīnyǔ).* The object is the receiver of the action of the verb.

Onomatopoeia — *Also known as: 象声词 (xiàngshēngcí) and 拟声词 (nǐshēngcí).* Onomatopoeia are words which represent sounds and noises.

Ordinal number — *Also known as: 序数词 (xùshù cí).* Ordinal numbers are numbers used to express rank or sequence. Think "1st," "2nd," etc. Ordinal numbers contrast with cardinal numbers.

Particle — *Also known as: 助词 (zhùcí).* Particles are function words that depend on other words or phrases to impart meaning. They're kind of like prepositions, but more abstract. In Chinese, the key ones are aspectual particles (for indicating aspect), structural particles (for indicating relationships between words), and modal particles (for indicating mood). Chinese particles are also special words because they tend to always take the neutral tone.

Passive voice — *Also known as: 被动结构 (bèidòng jiégòu), 被动句式 (bèidòng jùshì), 被动语态 (bèidòng yǔtài) and the passive.* "Passive voice" is a grammatical term used to refer to sentences in which the "recipient" of an action (often referred to as the "direct object" or simply "object") becomes the subject of the sentence, and the "doer" of the action is demoted to secondary importance or omitted altogether.

Passive structure — See **passive voice**

Personal pronoun — *Also known as: 人称代词 (rénchēng dàicí).* Personal pronouns include 我 (wǒ), 你 (nǐ), 他 (tā), and 她 (tā). To make them plural, all you need to do is add the suffix -们 (-men) to them. There is also a polite second person form 您 (nín), which cannot normally take the -们 (-men) suffix.

Place noun — *Also known as: 处所名词 (chùsuǒ míngcí).* Place nouns are nouns describing the position or place of something.

Place adverb — *Also known as: 处所副词 (chùsuǒ fùcí), location adverb, adverb of place and adverb of location.* Place adverbs modify the location of a verbs or adjective.

Placement verb — See **existential verb**

Phrase — *Also known as: 短语 (duǎnyǔ) and 词组 (cízǔ).* A phrase is a group of words that expresses a concept. It can be focused on fleshing out a particular word, as in a noun phrase or verb phrase. See also clause, which expresses a more complete thought.

Possessive pronoun — *Also known as: 物主代词 (wùzhǔ dàicí).* Possessive pronouns take the place of a noun and show ownership.

Potential complement — Verbs can take potential complements to indicate whether or not an action is possible. Potential complements contain a 得 (de) or a 不 (bu) immediate after the verb being modified, and are quite common in everyday spoken Mandarin.

Predicate — *Also known as: 谓语 (wèiyǔ).* Predicates are the main verb or verb phrase of a sentence, and state something about the subject. Aside from verbs, adjectives and sometimes even nouns can be predicates as well.

Preposition — *Also known as: 介词 (jiècí).* Prepositions are words that indicate location or direction. They are called "pre"-positions because they are positioned *before* the words that they modify.

Prepositional phrase — *Also known as: 介词短语 (jiècí duǎnyǔ).* A prepositional phrase is a phrase beginning with a preposition that precedes the word it modifies and clarifies that word's relationship with another word in the sentence.

Pronoun — *Also known as: 代词 (dàicí).* Pronouns substitute in for regular nouns and proper nouns to avoid unnecessary repetition of the same words over and over again.

Proper noun — *Also known as: 专有名词 (zhuānyǒu míngcí).* A proper noun is specific person, place or thing. Proper nouns are generally capitalized (e.g. Anubis, Asgard, AllSet Learning), both in English and in pinyin.

Psychological verb — *Also known as: 心理动词 (xīnlǐ dòngcí) and psych verb.* A psychological verb is a verb that conveys the speaker's mental state or attitude.

Qualitative adjective — *Also known as: 性质形容词 (xìngzhì xíngróngcí).* Qualitative adjectives describe the quality or nature of something.

Quantitative phrase — *Also known as: 数量短语 (shùliàng duǎnyǔ).* Quantitative phrases express a measurement of amount.

Quantity complement — *Also known as: 数量补语 (shùliàng bǔyǔ), quantitative complement and complement of quantity.* A quantity complement follows a verb and supplies information regarding an amount.

Question pronoun — See **question word**

Question word — *Also known as: 疑问代词 (yíwèn dàicí), question pronoun, interrogative pronoun.* A **question word** refers to a special kind of pronoun used to ask questions. These would include 什么 (shénme), 什么时候 (shénme shíhou), 谁 (shéi), 哪儿 (nǎr) / 哪里 (nǎlǐ), 哪个 (nǎge), 为什么 (wèishénme), 怎么 (zěnme). Beginners should pay attention to the placement of question words.

Reduplication — It is one of the great ironies of linguistics that the term for repeating a word is overly repetitive itself. You'd think that the word "duplication" would work just fine, but the linguistic term really is reduplication. In Chinese, verbs and adjectives are often reduplicated.

Relational verb — See **judgment verb**

Result complement — *Also known as: 结果补语 (jiéguǒ bǔyǔ), complement of result, resultative complement and result compound.* Result complements are a kind of verbal complement that appears very frequently in Chinese. Surprisingly enough, they're used to describe the result of a verb.

Scope adverb — *Also known as: 范围副词 (fànwéi fùcí).* Scope adverbs modify and expand a verb or adjective.

Sentence with a nominal predicate — See **nominal predicate sentence**

Sentence with a verbal predicate — *Also known as: 动词谓语句 (dòngcí wèiyǔ jù).* A sentence with a verb as the main element of its predicate is called a sentence with a verbal predicate. This type of sentence is extremely common.

Sentence with an adjectival predicate — See **adjectival predicate sentence**

Sentence with a subject-predicate structure as predicate — *Also known as: 主谓谓语句 (zhǔ-wèi wèiyǔ jù).*

Sentence-final particle — See **modal particle**

Sentential particle — See **modal particle**

Separable verb — *Also known as: 离合词 (líhécí) and verb-object phrase.* "Separable verbs" get their name from their ability to "separate" into two parts (a verb part and an object part), with other words in between. In fact, you could also simply call separable verbs "verb-object phrases."

Subject — *Also known as: 主语 (zhǔyǔ).* A subject is a noun or pronoun that the sentence centers around. It is the actor of the verb and is what something is said about.

Subject-predicate construction — *Also known as: 主谓结构 (zhǔ-wèi jiégòu).* The subject-predicate construction consists of a subject and a predicate, and may be part of a larger sentence, or may serve as a sentence on its own.

Subject-predicate sentence — *Also known as: 主谓句 (zhǔ-wèi jù).* A sentence composed of a subject and a predicate. The vast majority of sentences fit this description.

Subordinate clause — See **dependent clause**

State complement — *Also known as: 状态补语 (zhuàngtài bǔyǔ), 情态补语 (qíngtài bǔyǔ) and complement of state.* State complements describe an achieved state of an action. State complements are usually adjective phrases (adverb + adjective) but can take the form of verb phrases, subject-predicate phrases, or other complements. State complements that are adjective phrases often look the same as degree complements and thus are often lumped together with degree complements in textbooks.

Stative adjective — *Also known as: 状态形容词 (zhuàngtài xíngróngcí).* A stative adjective is an adjective describing a relatively unchanging or permanent condition/state.

Stative verb — *Also known as: 状态动词 (zhuàngtài dòngcí), 静态动词 (jìngtài dòngcí), state verb and static verb.* A stative verb is a verb describing a relatively unchanging or permanent condition/state. Stative verbs in Mandarin are usually translated as adjectives in English.

Structural particle — *Also known as: 结构助词 (jiégòu zhùcí).* A structural particle is a function word that denotes the structural/grammatical relationship between elements of a sentence.

Time adverb — *Also known as: 时间副词 (shíjiān fùcí).* Adverbs of time express the when, how long, or how often of a verb.

Time phrase — *Also known as: 时间短语 (shíjiān duǎnyǔ).* A time phrase occurs before the verb phrase and indicates the when, how long, or how often of a situation.

Time noun — *Also known as: 时间名词 (shíjiān míngcí), 时间词 (shíjiāncí), time nominal and temporal noun.* Time nouns are nouns that provide information regarding time. One reason they're noteworthy in Chinese is that words indicating time in English are often adverbs, whereas their Chinese counterparts are nouns.

Time-measure complement — *Also known as: 时量补语 (shí-liàng bǔyǔ).* Time-measure complements show the state or duration of an action.

Tone adverb — See **modal adverb**

Topic-comment structure — *Also known as: 主题句 (zhǔtí-jù), 主题结构 (zhǔtí jiégòu), 主题评论结构 (zhǔtí-pínglùn jiégòu), 主题述题结构 (zhǔtí-shùtí jiégòu) and 主题评述结构 (zhǔtí-píngshù jiégòu).* A topic-comment structure is an alternative to the typical subject-predicate sentence structure, whereby a topic (or theme) is followed by the speaker's comment on that topic. The topic is not the "doer" (subject) of the sentence, but rather sets the scope of the comments (some thoughts related to the topic).

Transitive verb — *Also known as: 及物动词 (jíwù dòngcí).* A transitive verb is an verb which takes a direct object.

Verb — *Also known as: 动词 (dòngcí).* Verbs are the "action" words which make up the predicates of most sentences, but may also simply indicate relationships, changes, or mental activity rather than physical actions. Verbs may take objects, and can also be reduplicated in Chinese. They can be negated, as well as modified by particles.

Verb measure word — *Also known as: 动量词 (dòng liàngcí), verbal measure word and verbal classifier.* A verb measure word accompanies the number of times a verb occurred to count the frequency or re-occurrence of an action. See: Measure words for verbs

Verb phrase — *Also known as: 动词性短语 (dòngcí-xìng duǎnyǔ) and verbal phrase.* A verb phrase is a phrase with a verb as a head word that has any sort of modifier. It commonly includes modal verbs before it and objects after it.

Verbal measure word — *Also known as: 动量补语 (dòng-liàng bǔyǔ), verb measure word, verbal classifier and action-measure complement.* This type of measure word is not used to count nouns. Rather, it is placed after verbs to show the frequency of an action.

Verbal predicate sentence — See **sentence with a verbal predicate**

Acknowledgments

The Chinese Grammar Wiki may have been pioneered by AllSet Learning, but it would not be possible without the hard work of many selfless individuals, including AllSet Learning interns, students, teachers, and regular users. Thank you!

AllSet Interns

• Donna Yee • Lucas Simons • Hugh Grigg • Greg McAndrews • Jonathan Pope • Pavel Dvorak • Parry Cadwallader • Jack Overstreet • Dan Emery • Erick Garcia • Mei Tong • Ben Slye • Brandon Sanchez • Logan Pauley • Ashlyn Weber • Michelle Birkenfeldt • Zach Herzog • Jazlyn Akaka • Salomé Vergne • Natalie Kuan • Jack Du • Erick Garcia • Cai Qingyang • Michael Moore • Liza Fowler • Mike Blood • Jacob Rodgers • Dominic Pote • Amani Core • Michelle Guerra • Amanda Gilbride • Callan Mossman • Jenna Salisbury • Audrey Brady • Jocelyn Kwong • Natalia Tun • Jake Liu

Volunteer Editors

Some of these editors did tons of work on their own, while others emailed in issues they found. We thank them all for the hard work and valuable contributions!

• Nicholas Fiorentini • Noémi Németh • Betsy • HuaWei • Kryby • Jay • Luolimao • Trackpick • Morris • Philip Harding • Gintaras Valentukonis • Benedikt Rauh

AllSet Teachers and Staff

• 马丽华 (Mǎ Lìhuá) • 李炯 (Lǐ Jiǒng) • 陈世霜 (Chén Shìshuāng) • 刘倖倖 (Liú Xìngxìng) • 赵以华 (Zhào Yǐhuá) • 于翠 (Yú Cuì) • 杨仁君 (Yáng Rénjùn) • 毛思平 (Máo Sīpíng) • 吴蒙蒙 (Wú Méngméng) • 贾贝茜 (Jiǎ Bèixī) • Parry Cadwallader • Michael Moore • John Pasden

Big props also go to full-time staff 李炯 (Lǐ Jiǒng) and 马丽华 (Mǎ Lìhuá) for their unflinching dedication to repeated proofreading tasks as we completed the final checks of the print book.

Sincere thanks to Parry Cadwallader for making both the original wiki itself as well as the ebook version of the Chinese Grammar Wiki possible technically, with very little extra production work needed from the academic team. A big thank you also to Adam Abrams for all the layout work that went into creating the print version.

Other Credits

The Chinese Grammar Wiki website and ebook both make use of the **Silk** icon set **FamFamFam.com**. The Chinese Grammar Wiki BOOK (print edition) uses a "structure" icon from **Pixeden.com**, as well as several icons from **Icomoon.io**. The HSK Grammar series uses graphics from Pablo Stanley's outstanding **Humaaans** vector art library.

References

This page is a bibliography for the Chinese Grammar Wiki. It lists all sources referenced extensively when researching the content of the Chinese Grammar Wiki grammar points.

- Chen, Ru 陈如, and Xiaoya Zhu 朱晓亚. *Hanyu Changyong Geshi 330 Li 汉语常用格式 330 例 [Common Chinese Patterns 330]*. Beijing: Beijing Foreign Languages Printing House, 2010. Print.
- Fang, Yuqing 房玉清. *Shiyong Hanyu Yufa 实用汉语语法 [A Practical Chinese Grammar]*. Beijing: Beijing Yuyan Daxue Chubanshe, 2008. Print.
- General Information on the HSK. *Hanyu Kaoshi Fuwu Wang*, http://www.chinesetest.cn. Web.
- Herzberg, Qin Xue, and Larry Herzberg. *Basic Patterns of Chinese Grammar: A Student's Guide to Correct Structures and Common Errors*. Berkeley, CA: Stone Bridge, 2011. Print.
- Ho, Yong. *Intermediate Chinese*. New York: Hippocrene, 2004. Print.
- Jiang Liping 姜丽萍, ed. Wang Fang 王芳, Wang Feng 王枫, and Liu Liping 刘丽萍. *标准课程 Standard Course: HSK 1*. Beijing: Beijing Language and Culture University Press, 2014. Print.
- Jiang Liping 姜丽萍, ed. Wang Feng 王枫, Liu Liping 刘丽萍, and Wang Fang 王芳. *标准课程 Standard Course: HSK 2*. Beijing: Beijing Language and Culture University Press, 2014. Print.
- Jiang Liping 姜丽萍, ed. Yu Miao 于淼, and Li Lin 李琳. *标准课程 Standard Course: HSK 3*. Beijing: Beijing Language and Culture University Press, 2014. Print.
- Jiang Liping 姜丽萍, ed. Dong Zheng 董政 and Zhang Jun 张军. *标准课程 Standard Course: HSK 4 上*. Beijing: Beijing Language and Culture University Press, 2014. Print.
- Jiang Liping 姜丽萍, ed. Zhang Jun 张军 and Dong Zheng 董政. *标准课程 Standard Course: HSK 4 下*. Beijing: Beijing Language and Culture University Press, 2014. Print.
- Jiang Liping 姜丽萍, ed. Liu Chang 刘畅 and 鲁江 Lu Jiang. *标准课程 Standard Course: HSK 5 上*. Beijing: Beijing Language and Culture University Press, 2014. Print.
- Jiang Liping 姜丽萍, ed. 鲁江 Lu Jiang and Liu Chang 刘畅. *标准课程 Standard Course: HSK 5 下*. Beijing: Beijing Language and Culture University Press, 2015. Print.
- Jiang Liping 姜丽萍, ed. Yao Shujun 么书君 and Yang Huizhen 杨慧真. *标准课程 Standard Course: HSK 6 上*. Beijing: Beijing Language and

Culture University Press, 2015. Print.

- Jiang Liping 姜丽萍, ed. Yang Huizhen 杨慧真 and Yao Shujun 么书君. *标准课程 Standard Course: HSK 6 下*. Beijing: Beijing Language and Culture University Press, 2016. Print.
- Li, Charles N., and Sandra A. Thompson. *Mandarin Chinese: A Functional Reference Grammar*. Berkeley: U of California, 1981. Print.
- Li, Dejin 李德津, and Meizhen Cheng 程美珍, eds. *Waiguoren Shiyong Hanyu Yufa 外国人实用汉语语法 [A Practical Chinese Grammar for Foreigners]*. Beijing: Beijing Yuyan Daxue Chubanshe, 1998. Print.
- Li, Luxing 李禄兴, Ling Zhang 张玲, and Juan Zhang 张娟. *Hanyu Yufa Baixiang Jianglian: Chuzhongji 汉语语法百项讲练：初中级 [Chinese Grammar–Broken Down Into 100 Items]*. Beijing: Beijing Language and Culture UP, 2011. Print.
- Li, Xiaoqi 李晓琪, ed. *Xiandai Hanyu Xuci Shouce 现代汉语虚词手册 [Modern Chinese Function Words Handbook]: A Guide to Function Words in Modern Chinese*. Beijing: Beijing Daxue Chubanshe, 2003. Print.
- Liu, Delian 刘德联, and Xiaoyu Liu 刘晓雨. *Hanyu Kouyu Changyong Jushi Lijie 汉语口语常用句式例解 [Exemplification of Common Sentence Patterns in Spoken Chinese]*. Ed. Liwen Song 宋立文. Beijing: Beijing Daxue Chubanshe, 2005. Print.
- Liu, Xun 刘珣, ed. *Xin Shiyong Hanyu Keben 新实用汉语课本 [New Practical Chinese Reader Textbook 1]*. Beijing: Beijing Language and Culture UP, 2002. Print.
- Liu, Xun 刘珣. *Xin Shiyong Hanyu Keben 新实用汉语课本 [New Practical Chinese Reader Textbook 2]*. Beijing: Beijing Language and Culture UP, 2002. Print.
- Liu, Xun 刘珣. *Xin Shiyong Hanyu Keben 新实用汉语课本 [New Practical Chinese Reader Textbook 3]*. Beijing: Beijing Language and Culture UP, 2003. Print.
- Liu, Yuehua 刘月华, Wenyu Pan 潘文娱, and Wei Gu 故桦. *Shiyong Xiandai Hanyu Yufa 实用现代汉语语法 [Practical Modern Chinese Grammar]*. Beijing: Shangwu Yinshuguan Chuban, 2001. Print.
- Liu, Yuehua, and Tao-chung Yao. *Zhongwen Tingshuo Duxie 中文听说读写 [Integrated Chinese Textbook Simplified Characters Level 1 Part 2]*. 3rd ed. Boston: Cheng & Tsui, 2009. Print.
- Liu, Yuehua, and Tao-chung Yao. *Zhongwen Tingshuo Duxie 中文听说读写 [Integrated Chinese Textbook Simplified Characters Level 2 Part 2]*. 3rd ed. Boston: Cheng & Tsui, 2009. Print.
- Liu, Yuehua, and Tao-chung Yao. *Zhongwen Tingshuo Duxie 中文听说读写 [Integrated Chinese Textbook Simplified Characters Level 1 Part 1]*.

3rd ed. Boston: Cheng & Tsui, 2009. Print.

- Liu, Yuehua, and Tao-chung Yao. *Zhongwen Tingshuo Duxie 中文听说读写 [Integrated Chinese Textbook Simplified Characters Level 2* **Part** *1]*. 3rd ed. Boston: Cheng & Tsui, 2009. Print.
- Lü, Shuxiang 吕叔湘, comp. *Xiandai Hanyu Babai Ci 现代汉语八百词 [800 Modern Chinese Words]*. Beijing: Shangwu Yinshuguan, 1980. Print.
- Ma, Jing-heng Sheng, and Claudia Ross. *Modern Mandarin Chinese Grammar: A Practical Guide*. London: Routledge, 2006. Print.
- Mu, Ling, Rongzhen Li, and Peisong Xu. *Chinese Usage Dictionary*. Center for Language Study, Yale University, 2004. Web.
- "Qingwen." Podcast audio content. *ChinesePod*. Web.
- Ross, Claudia. *Schaum's Outline of Chinese Grammar*. New York: McGraw-Hill, 2004. Print.
- Teng, Wen-Hua. *Yufa!: A Practical Guide to Mandarin Chinese Grammar*. London: Hodder Education, 2011. Print.
- *Xiandai Hanyu Xuci Lishi 现代汉语虚词例释 [Modern Chinese Function Words Examples and Explanations]*. Beijing: Shangwu Yinshuguan, 1957. Print.
- Yip, Po-ching, and Don Rimmington. *Chinese: An Essential Grammar*. London: Routledge, 1997. Print.
- Yip, Po-ching, Don Rimmington, Xiaoming Zhang, and Rachel Henson. *Basic Chinese: A Grammar and Workbook*. London: Routledge, 1998. Print.
- Zhang, Jing 张婧, ed. *Yufa Jingjiang Jinglian 语法精讲精练 [Practicing HSK Grammar]*. 1st ed. Beijing: Sinolingua, 2008. Print.
- Zhu, Xiaoxing 朱晓星, ed. *Jianming Hanyu Yufa Xuexi Shouce 简明汉语语法学习手册 [Simple Chinese Grammar Study Handbook]: Chinese Grammar without Tears*. Beijing: Beijing Daxue Chubanshe, 2002. Print.

Printed in Poland
by Amazon Fulfillment
Poland Sp. z o.o., Wrocław